On The Bandera Frontier

Contributions to the
Bandera County Historian 1992-2010

Earl S. Hardin, Jr.

On The Bandera Frontier

Contributions to the
Bandera County Historian 1992-2010

Earl S. Hardin, Jr.

All Rights Reserved

No part of this book may be reproduced, transmitted or downloaded in any form or by any means, electronic or mechanical, including copying, photocopying, recording or by any information storage and retrieval system without written permission from the author, except for the inclusion of brief quotations in a review.

ISBN: 9781944071752

Copyright   2019   Earl S. Hardin, Jr.

Contents

1	Bandera Pass	11
2	The Frio Water Hole	13
3	Amasa Clark, Coons' Train and The U.S. Boundary Commission	17
4	John James	23
5	John Hunter Herndon	29
6	Charles de Montel	33
7	The Lymon Wight Colony	39
8	The Indian On The White Horse	41
9	Contemporary Newspaper Articles	49
10	The Mary Davis Petition	51
11	Wherever They May Be Found: Controversy and Consequences of The Callahan Raid, 1855	53
12	The Petition To Form Bandera County	65
13	The First County Election Results	69
14	U.S. Army Posts In The Bandera Region	71
15	Jose Policarpio Rodriguez	85
16	Keeping The Camels: The Camel Handlers of Camp Verde	97
17	Ballantyne's Rangers 1860	105
18	The Secession Vote On The West Texas Frontier	111
19	Paul's Company and The Taking of Camp Verde	113
20	E.M. Downs, M.D.	121
21	Charles Montague Letter	133
22	Bandera Resolutions 1861	137
23	The Bandera Home Guardes	139
24	Diphtheria On The Civil War Texas Frontier	147

25	The Incident at San Julian Creek	155
26	The Bandera Resolutions 1863	163
27	Three Letters and A Crisis	165
28	The Frontier Organization	173
29	The Last Campaign	185
30	Frank Buckelew	191
31	Sheriffs and Rangers	201
32	The Life Story of Mrs. Annie E. Brown Revisited	215
33	Terror In The Afternoon: The 1881 Frio Canyon Raid	221
34	The Maudslay Academy	229
35	Jailbreak	235
36	Bulah, the "Lost" County and The Panic of 1893	241
37	Julius Real: A Son of The Hill Country 1890-1944	243
38	The Woman of The Western Star	249

1

Bandera Pass

A U.S. Army officer in the early 1850s described Bandera Pass as "the most dangerous location in Texas." Legends of battles fought there extend back to the Spanish colonial times. According to one legend, General Bandera defeated Apache Indians there. Another more persistent legend states that banners (*banderas*) were placed at the pass to mark a treaty boundary. Captain Jose de Urrutia, leading a troop of Spanish soldiers in 1739, may have been the European discoverer of *La Puerta de la Bandera*.

The upper portions of the Guadalupe and Medina rivers are separated by a rough ridge of steep hills with no easy passage other than Bandera Pass. Fifty to seventy-five feet lower than the surrounding hills, it is about 100 yards wide and 500 yards long. South of the pass, the rivers and creeks that drain from the area of Bandera County form wide canyons through the hills, opening onto rolling prairie from which Indian raiders could spread out through the settlements.

Jack Hays and his company of Texas Rangers patrolled the region in the early 1840s. After Texas became a state of the Union in 1845, ranger companies were sent to the region at various times, including Callahan's Rangers for a couple of months in 1855.

From 1856 through 1869, camels could be seen grazing along the slopes leading to the pass. The U.S. Army established the easternmost base of its camel experiment on Verde Creek just north of the pass. Camp Verde was also home to a company of the 2nd U.S. Cavalry, which provided some security for the region until the Civil War.

Ranger companies were stationed at Camp Verde during most of the Civil War years. The U.S. Cavalry briefly returned to Camp Verde after the war, but the region's settlers suffered from a lack of frontier protection during most of the Reconstruction years. A.J. Sowell tells the story of Jack Hardy, a young man who was captured by 15 Comanches as they raided through Kerr County in 1870. They continued south through Bandera Pass:

> From this point the Indians took the Bandera road and after darkness fell, passed through the town, two and two abreast, and crossed the Medina River. They stole a horse at the edge of town.

The Frontier Force was established in 1870 and the men of Company C under Captain John Samson were the last rangers to be stationed at Camp Verde. By 1874 when the Frontier Battalion was organized, ranger patrols were generally more to the north and west of Bandera Pass. The military importance of the pass declined and was overshadowed by its more domestic importance to wagon freighters and cattle drivers. The pass is traversed today by State Highway 173.

2

The Frio Water Hole

The Frio Water Hole is near the head of the Frio River in the area that became Real County in 1913, but was part of Bandera County from 1856 until the organization of Edwards County in 1883. The river often runs dry and the Frio Water Hole is the only source of water for miles around. The site was well known to Indians and Texas Rangers.

A.J. Sowell accounts tell of the Lipan Apaches under Chief Juan Castro who lived for many years on Francisco Perez Creek in what is now Medina County. Henri Castro established Castroville just north of the Indian camp in 1844. By 1848, as more settlers moved into the area, the Lipan Apaches found their position untenable and moved out to the Frio Water Hole and began raiding the settlements. The following year Big Foot Wallace and Ed Westfall, leading a group of Medina County men, defeated Juan Castro's band.

As the Texas frontier continued to expand, life became more difficult for Indians attempting to live between the line of settlements and the Comanche Barrier. The Lipan Apaches under Juan Castro at the Frio Water Hole and others under Chiquito and Chipote near Fredericksburg moved into Mexico in 1854 rather than move onto the Texas reservation on the Brazos River. With other Lipan Apache leaders already in Mexico, including Costilietos, they established a raiding route from a crossing near San Felipe (Del Rio) on the Rio Grande through a gap in the line of U.S. Army forts between Fort Clark and Fort McKavett. (Fort Territt had been established in the gap in 1852, but was closed the following year.) The Indian raiders from Mexico or the Pecos or Devil's rivers passed through the corridor formed by the headwaters of the South Llano and the Nueces rivers. Through this corridor they would reach the Frio Water Hole. From there they could raid north, east, or south into the early West Texas settlements. By crossing a treacherous trail over the rough divide between the Frio River and the Sabinal River, they could descend into the Lost Maples area from which they could raid down the Sabinal or Medina rivers or through the canyons formed by Seco and Hondo creeks.

In 1861, in the midst of the secession turmoil, the A.J. Sowell accounts tell, a Comanche raid involved nearly 200 warriors racing through the settlements resulting in a half-dozen or more people killed from Bandera to Atascosa County. The various raiding parties regrouped into two large bands of nearly 100 men apiece as they returned to the north. One group went up the Sabinal River, perhaps ascending the winding route over the Medina/Guadalupe divide that is today State Highway 16, before heading out to the Devil's River pursued by Seco Smith and some Medina County men and some rangers. The other group of raiders went up Seco Creek pursued by Big Foot Wallace with some Medina and Atascosa County men. The Comanches laid a successful ambush in the high ground above the headwaters of Seco Creek and a desperate fight ensued. Eventually the Comanches withdrew with their horse herd and the battered militiamen retired to the Ware Settlement to tend to their wounded and gather more men. Captain Wallace then made a determined effort to beat the Indian raiders to the trail over the divide that led to the Frio Water Hole. The effort was successful and an ambush set up, but one of Wallace's men fired his rifle too soon and the Indians scattered. The militiamen recovered close to 200 horses.

R.H. Williams, riding with the Partizan Rangers (Confederate troops) in 1862 in pursuit of Union men who were following the Indian trails to Mexico, described the horse trail over the rough terrain:

> It was, for the most part, desperate country to ride over, for we were well in the mountains, and frequently had to dismount and lead our horses down rocky slides. Towards evening the trail led us to a large water-hole on the head of the Frio River; perhaps the only one to be found for many miles of its course, which showed the enemy had good guides. Here we watered our thirsty horses and filled our canteens and, after a brief rest, pushed on again.

October 27, 1870, Captain John Sanson, commanding Company C of the Frontier Force (Texas Rangers), made this report from Camp Verde to the adjutant general:

> In twenty minutes after I got word of the Indians [October 4th] Sargeant Nelson & seven men were on the march with orders to travel the entire night & all next day in order to get in front of the Indians at one of their watering places, generally known as the Frio Water Hole and to remain there four days, then strike for Paint Creek (waters of Llano) to meet me with supplies.

Sergeant Lewis Nelson made this report:

> My men & I rode the entire night of the 4th inst and the next day until night without stopping more that a few minutes at a time; reached Frio Water Hole about night put out sentinels; no Indians seen or heard untill about 9 o'clock at night; then there was a noise made by the Indians something like cattle, So the next morning we looked out for a

trail. Found that the Indians had passed within four or six hundred yds. of Camp. We took the trail followed about four miles, came in sight of them; charged them, the Indians ran.

I ran them about fifteen miles, gaining distance on them all the time, and would have cought them but they ran into the cedar breaks of the Nueces, one in a place. There was but four Indians. I captured six head of saddle horses, and two mules. Four or five of the horses are Mr. Huebner's the bearer of the information that there was Indians in the country.

June and July 1874, Captain Neal Coldwell and Company F of the Frontier Battalion (Texas Rangers) patrolled the Indian corridor from "Camp Frio" at the Frio Water Hole. This company was temporarily disbanded, but quickly reformed to meet the threat of lawlessness in the area. The U.S. Army had greatly reduced Indian raids from Mexico; however, outlaws were taking over the Indian raiding routes causing great consternation among Hill Country citizens, particularly in Kerr County. Major Jones, in charge of the Frontier Battalion, took his escort company, a detachment of Company F, and a minuteman ranger company from Comfort to sweep the area. That was the end of the South Fork Clan, perhaps the largest organized outlaw band ever to operate in the region. There were still problems with smaller outlaw bands or individuals over the next few years, but many of the outlaw element remaining were fugitives of justice from other areas trying to hide out on the frontier.

The last documented Indian raid into the Bandera region took place near the Frio Water Hole in 1881 when Lipan Apaches killed two people north of Leakey.

3

Amasa Clark, Coons' Train, and The U. S. Boundary Commission

In 1849, after the US-Mexican War, New York-born Amasa Clark was waiting for his discharge from the 3rd Infantry near El Paso del Norte, "While my company was waiting at San Elizario word came for us to go into the Guadalupe Mountains to the relief of Koonce's wagon train, which was hemmed in by a band of Indians." Between 70-80 Apaches had attacked the supply train of 15 men and 12 corn-laden wagons.

Benjamin Franklin Coons was a St. Louis merchant and freighter. He had made many trips along the Santa Fe Trail before purchasing a ranch along the Rio Grande in 1848. The following year in September, Major Jefferson Van Horne and four companies of the 3rd Infantry camped nearby and rented six acres of Coons' land. B.F. Coons took on the task of bringing up the army supplies from Indianola on the Texas coast.

Amasa Clark's discharge finally came through and he made his way to San Antonio where he took a job with the U.S. Army cleaning out the Alamo chapel to make way for quartermaster supplies. In the summer of 1850 he bought a herd of cattle and drove them out to the Quihi settlement in Medina County with the intention of starting a ranch. Ben Coons came by with a train of 340 freight wagons going out of San Antonio with supplies for the U.S. Army troops posted on his ranch. Finding a scarcity of willing and able wagon freighters in San Antonio, he accepted whomever he could get. He offered 25-year-old Clark a job.

Unlike the previous year's train, this one traveled with army protection. Brevet Major John T. Sprague, the temporary commandant at Fort Inge (near present day Uvalde), gathered three companies of mounted infantry and met the train at Las Moras Spring.

A few months after Coons' Train moved out from Quihi on the "southern" route to El Paso del Norte, the men of the U.S. Boundary Commission were starting out from Fredericksburg on the "northern" route. (Each route had its own southern and northern branches and variations.) It was a grueling journey either way: Water was scarce and hostile Indians could appear at any time. Both routes were relatively new and at that time were traveled mainly by army troops, army supply trains, and a few Forty-niners. The routes converged at the Pecos River, following that stream to the Guadalupe Mountains, passing under the peak of El Capitan, turning west towards Coons Rancho.

John Russell Bartlett was the U.S. Boundary Commissioner and traveled with about 30 men who served as interpreters, naturalists, and surveyors. Colonel John McClellan of the U.S. Topographical Engineers commanded the military escort. The men of the Boundary Commission reached Texas by way of the port of Indianola. They continued inland through Victoria and San Antonio. They were appalled by the prices they were charged for food and lodging along the way. Bartlett and 12 of his party stopped to buy a supply of corn and a wagon from Lymon Wight at the Mormon settlement of Zodiac (just before Fredericksburg). Staying for dinner, they were pleasantly surprised as Commissioner Bartlett noted, "The entire charge here for a dinner for twelve persons, and corn for as many animals, was three dollars—a modest demand, which strikingly contrasted with the Astor House prices of a Mr. McGrew, and some others, between Indianola and Victoria."

A few weeks after leaving Fredericksburg and civilization behind, the Commission members had a friendly meeting with some Lipan Apaches and their leaders, Chipote and Chiquito. Some weeks later they were prudent enough not to try making contact with the Comanches they saw in the distance. The warriors were riding up their famous War Trail, returning from raids in Mexico. Major Robert H. Emory with the military escort estimated the Comanche force at around 400 and their herd of Mexican horses at around 1000.

The Commission party consisted of a mule-drawn carriage and a few wagons with most of the men on horseback. They sometimes exceeded 30 miles a day. They made remarkable time compared to the men of Coons' Train. The ox-drawn freight wagons did well if they made 15 miles a day. The 60-70 teamsters rode in the wagons or walked beside them while some drove a herd of 500 cattle as well as other assorted livestock. It was a difficult journey and several men and quite a few cattle and oxen dropped dead along the way. Some wagons broke down or were left without oxen to pull them and had to be abandoned.

By October the teamsters had reached the Guadalupe Mountains with between 60-120 wagons and still had 100 miles to go. The last six-day stretch was a dry one and they could not carry enough water for all the men and animals. They waited several weeks for rain which did not come, then sent a messenger ahead to have barrels of water set out for them along the rest of the way.

Major Van Horne, commanding the post at Coons' Ranch, wrote to headquarters September 1st that he understood some of his supplies might reach him in ten days, but "the remainder God knows when. The oxen are perishing and Coons' train is in wretched condition, he [Coons] himself doubtful whether it will ever reach here."

November 10, John Bartlett and an advance party from the Boundary Commission spotted smoke rising in the distance and with a telescope he discerned "many wagons stretching over the plain" below the mountains and along a spring-fed pond. "Ragged, dirty and unshaven" teamsters surrounded the Commission members as they rode into the camp. Both parties were glad to meet up with people from the "States."

Amasa Clark remembered the occasion: "While we were in this camp the U.S. Boundary Surveying party came along with fat teams, and the men were all dressed in style. They camped near us for several days. These were the first people we had seen since we left Quihi. One of our men went over to their camp to talk to them and learn how things were happening back in the settlements. When he came back a man named Hankinson asked him what he had learned, and he replied, 'Victoria is sunk.' Hankinson decided to go to the camp and get full particulars, and I went along with him. When Hankinson walked up he asked one of the officers if it was true about Victoria being sunk. 'Yes,' he said, 'it sunk my purse for about $300."

The men of the Boundary Commission continued their journey, mapping the new boundary between the U.S. and Mexico from the Rio Grande to the Pacific Ocean. After nearly five months of hardship, Coons' Train finally reached the army post near the end of November.

As the U.S. Army sorted out its troops to more permanent locations, the soldiers at Coons Rancho were transferred in 1851. The loss of income, combined with other business reversals, bankrupted Coons. Amasa Clark recalled, "Mr. Koonce, owner of the wagon train, was broke and could not pay his men the twenty-five dollars per month promised." Benjamin Franklin Coons moved on to California, but the settlement that grew up around the troop camp at Coons Rancho became known as Franklin. Today the location is downtown El Paso.

Clark made a few more freighting trips to the El Paso region. Eventually he settled in Bandera County. In the early 1920s, when the old-time wagon freighters organized the Pioneer Freighters' Association, they appointed Amasa Clark Honorary Vice-president for life.

Sources

Bartlett, John Russell. Personal Narrative of Explorations and Incidents of Texas, New Mexico, California, Sonora, and Chihuahua, Connected With The United States and Mexican Boundary Commission, During The Years 1850, 51, 52, and 53. D. Applton and Company. 1854.

Clark, Amasa Gleason. Reminiscences of a Centenarian. Naylor Company. San Antonio. 1930.

Cox, Mike. "The Comanche War Trail: Terror In The Night." Texas Highways. Volume 44. Number 8. (August 1997) Pages 42-50.

Cremony, John C. Life Among the Apaches. Commercial Herald Office. San Francisco. 1868.

Pingenot, Ben E. "The Great Wagon Train Expedition of 1850." The Southwestern Historical Quarterly. Volume 98. Number 2. (October 1994) Pages 184-225.

Smith, Thomas T. The Old Army In Texas: A Research Guide To The U.S. Army In Nineteenth-century Texas. Texas State Historical Association. Austin. 1996.

Timmons, W.H. "American El Paso: The Formative years, 1848-1854." <u>The Southwestern Historical Quarterly</u>. Volume 87. Number 1. (July 1983) Pages 1-36.

Tyler, Ron, et al, eds. <u>The New Handbook of Texas</u>. Texas State Historical Association. Austin. 1996.

4

John James

John James came from a long line of British military men. While he spent his childhood in Nova Scotia, Canada, where his father was stationed, John was born in England in 1819 where his parents had returned for a visit. In 1836, when he was 17, he heard about the Texas Revolution and set out to continue the family tradition. He became ill in Vicksburg and, upon recovering, worked a short time for a merchant who had taken him in. The man recognized John's enterprising abilities and offered him a partnership, but the young man was still determined to have his adventure in Texas.

Eighteen-year-old John James reached San Antonio, the western edge of the Texas frontier, in 1837. Ludovic Colquhon needed someone to manage his land business while he made a trip of several months to the east. John James, too late for the war, took the job.

Land speculation was a major enterprise in Texas. The Texas army veterans were paid in land, much of which was in the Bexar Territories, all the land west of San Antonio to the Rio Grande River and north to the panhandle. People of European descent simply did not live in that region at this time since it lay in the path of Comanche raiders. Many veterans sold their land to speculators. These tracts of land had to be located and surveyed. This was done by the Bexar County surveyors under Robert Hays, brother of the Texas Ranger captain, Jack Hays. John James took up surveying and became acquainted with another young Assistant Bexar County Surveyor and future James partner, Charles de Montel.

John James developed his own land business, purchasing land from Martin Hardin in 1838 and acquiring a headright of 320 acres in 1839. At the same time he continued the dangerous business of surveying for Bexar County. In 1839 Indians attacked his surveying party on the Frio River. Five of his men were killed. After that incident, the surveyors were escorted by several Texas Rangers.

On March 19, 1840, John James was present for the event that became known as The Court House Fight. Some of the Penateka Comanches had come into San Antonio for treaty negotiations when a misunderstanding led to a tragic fight in which many people were killed. In the melee, an Indian lunged at John James with a knife, but his life was saved when Jim Dunn pulled him back and shot the Indian through the head.

In 1842, the Mexican Army made two invasions into Texas in response to the Texan's Santa Fe Expedition and to maintain the Mexican claim on Texas. The second invasion took place in September 1842, when General Adrian Woll commanding 1000 Mexican soldiers held San Antonio for several days before heading back for Mexico. Jack Hays and Matthew Caldwell followed after the Mexican force with Texas militia that included John James in the ranks.

The Mexican army, repulsed at the Battle of Salado, withdrew into Mexico along with 67 prisoners taken in San Antonio and some very important San Antonio archival material that included the surveying notes for property lines. John James knew the notes by memory. He resurveyed San Antonio and established new field notes for the records.

In 1843 Henri Castro began a land colonizing venture west of the Medina River that resulted in the towns of Castroville, Quihi, Vandenburg, and D'Hanis. John

James and Charles de Montel did most of the required surveying.

By 1847 John James was a prominent citizen in San Antonio and chief surveyor of Bexar County. That year, in August, he married Emaline Polley, daughter of an Old Three Hundred plantation owner. The following year Joseph Schmidt constructed a stone house for them on Commerce Street. It was one of the first two-story houses in the city and among the first to have a chimney and fireplace.

Emaline James died during the 1849 cholera epidemic. John James remarried in 1851 to Annie Milby of Brazoria County where her father was a respected plantation owner and Mason. She had three unmarried sisters who came to live in the James house which became a center of much social activity in the 1850s. U.S. military men who visited the James house on many occasions included Robert E. Lee, Albert Sidney Johnston, D.H. Vinton, Joseph E. Johnson, John B. Hood, Braxton Bragg, and Policarpo Rodriguez.

By this time John James' business activities were varied and extensive. Recently, James Sweet had married one of James' sisters in Nova Scotia and immigrated to Texas. In 1850 John James put up the capital for his brother-in-law to establish the James R. Sweet & Company mercantile store in San Antonio. The company continued successfully until the Civil War when James Sweet, a multi-term San Antonio mayor, joined the Confederate Army.

In 1852, John James entered a partnership with Gustav Theissen to speculate in some land along the upper reaches of Cibolo Creek about 50 miles northwest of San Antonio. They bought the land from Christian Hesse who had decided against settling there when his brother declined to join him. A town site was surveyed and named for a German political writer, Ludwig

Boerne. The Adelsverein, a German company formed to promote emigration to Texas, had gone bankrupt by this time, but Germans continued to move into the Texas Hill Country and Boerne became one of many German towns in the area.

That same year John James became partner to Charles de Montel and John H. Herndon to develop some of the unsettled land in the upper Medina River Valley. They began buying large tracts of land in the region and planned to work a saw mill in the area to take advantage of the cypress trees growing along the river. Cypress shingles and lumber were in great demand at that time. The town of Bandera City began with a few families of settlers in 1853.

In June 1854 John James trail bossed a herd of over 1,000 head of cattle to California where the 1849 Gold Rush had created a great demand for beef. His return trip was by ship to New York. He made a side trip to visit his childhood home of Bridgetown, Nova Scotia before returning to San Antonio in November 1855.

Meanwhile the population of the Bandera settlement fluctuated drastically as Indian raids increased. Nevertheless, the shingle and lumber industry took hold. The 1856 county tax records indicate activities in Bandera County by the firms of James, Montel & Hewitt and James, Montel & Herrington. John James opened a lumber yard in San Antonio to market the cypress products. According to Vinton Lee James,

> The firm was known as the Bandera Mills of James, Montel and Company. The lumber was hauled overland by horses and oxen to San Antonio. The lumber yard was the first in San Antonio, and was located on West Commerce Street. James built a hotel in Bandera.

Although John James was Episcopalian, he encouraged the activities of all faiths in Bandera. He donated lots for the Catholic and Methodist churches there.

By 1859 he owned or controlled 150,000 acres of land scattered across West Texas mostly in 160, 320, or 640 acre tracts. When the army decided on a location for a new fort, first at Fort Stockton and later at Fort Davis, they found the desired land they had chosen belonged to John James. The land for Fort Davis was leased to the army for 20 years at $1,000 per year.

Mr. James maintained a ranch in Bandera County and one in Uvalde County raising cattle and sheep. His horse brand was the running M and his cattle brand was "210." In 1860 he imported 500 Merino sheep and "some of the best rams money could buy" to his 3500 acre Bandera County ranch.

When the Civil War broke out John James was overweight for the regular army, but served in San Antonio's home guards. (Vinton Lee James described his father as being 5'9" tall and weighing 225 pounds.) He made a trip to Richmond during the war to lobby for Texas interests.

In 1869 John James moved his sheep from the Bandera County ranch to his Uvalde County ranch where Henry Shane was his partner. J.F. Weldon leased the Bandera County ranch for $100 a year and raised sheep there.

The Franco-Prussian War of 1870 gave the wool market a big boost. John James, who was very knowledgeable in animal husbandry, promoted the sheep industry and wrote many newspaper articles on the subject. He was a stockholder in the Comal Woolen Factory in New Braunfels and wore clothes made from the cloth produced there.

He was one of three bondsmen for the City of San Antonio's $300,000 bond for the Galveston, Harrisburg, and San Antonio Railway Company which completed the line to San Antonio on February 15, 1877. The first railroad to San Antonio was his last enterprise for he became ill in the spring and died November 26, 1877, 56 years old.

Vinton Lee James memorialized his father's character in the following paragraph;

> John James had the distinction during his life of conveying more land to settlers and different parties than any other man in Texas. Years ago it was common talk among business men in San Antonio that James knew the location of every permanent water hole in west Texas. The name of John James affixed to a deed conveying land was in itself a guarantee that the title was perfect, and to this day of all his numerous conveyances of land his reputation for honesty and correctness has never been questioned.

Sources

Bandera County Historian. Volume 1, Fall 1978 and Volume 11, 1988.

James, Vinton Lee. Frontier and Pioneer Recollections of Early Days in San Antonio and West Texas. Artes Graficas. San Antonio. 1938.

Chabot, Frederick C. Chabot. With the Makers of San Antonio: Genealogies of the Early Latin, Anglo-American, and German Families with Occasional Biographies. Artes Graficas. San Antonio. 1937.

5

John Hunter Herndon

John H. Herndon, born of wealthy parents in Scott County, Kentucky, July 8, 1813, was educated in arts and law at Transylvania College near Lexington, Kentucky. Shortly after graduating, he abandoned his fledgling Kentucky law practice and set out for Texas. He arrived in Galveston in January 1838, with several thousand dollars in his pocket and a fine wardrobe. He spent some months in Houston, acclimating himself to Houston society and culture while preparing for the Texas bar. He was elected to the position of engrossing clerk of the House of Representatives and a few months later moved to Richmond in Fort Bend County where he was admitted to the bar. August 27, 1839, he married Barbara Calvit, heiress to a Brazoria County sugar plantation.

John Herndon was a successful lawyer and soon was involved in all sorts of public and political matters in the Republic of Texas. His law practice involved cases in the district courts of the Second Judicial District and in the Supreme Court of Texas. He expanded his business interests in all directions of Antebellum Texas economics. He served a brief stint as a soldier in the 1842 Somervell Expedition.

By the 1850s, the Herndons, with four sons and one daughter, had moved to the Herndon Plantation in Brazoria County, while keeping a summer town house on the coast at Velasco. Known to the Calvits as Evergreen, the plantation was the richest of 46 in the county. A brick sugar house stood not far from the ten or twelve room, two-story frame house with a several-room office building in the yard. There was a stable of Arabian horses and herds of cattle, in addition to livestock on ranches in Medina, Guadalupe, and Matagorda counties.

A wedding in 1851 may have been the social catalyst for a Herndon business venture: John James of San Antonio married Annie Milby, daughter of Brazoria County plantation owners. The following year John Herndon and John James, with Charles de Montel of Castroville, formed the partnership of James, Montel & Company to develop real estate and mill cypress lumber and shingles in the area that became Bandera County. This was but one of many Herndon partnerships that were operating simultaneously throughout the state. A partnership with Medina County rancher, H.J. Richarz, for instance, involved sheep raising and breeding. By 1860, 46 years old, John Herndon was the wealthiest man in Texas with properties valued at $1,605,000 and personal property at $106,050. He owned 40 slaves.

A two-story stone structure built around 1860 on Bandera City's Main Street (11th Street today) was among the last projects of James, Montel & Company: The Civil War ended the partnership. Much of the Herndon fortune disappeared in Confederate notes and bonds during the war. He served as colonel of the Brazoria and Fort Bend county home guards and was president of the Buffalo Bayou, Brazos and Colorado Railway Company, an 80-mile line from Harrisburg to Alleyton. During this time he played a part in the drama involving Dr. Richard R. Peebles who had tended the wounded at the 1836 San Jacinto battle. Although a slaveholder, Dr. Peebles and four other men were arrested in October 1863 by General J.B. Magruder for distributing a pamphlet calling for an end to the war. A man named Baldwin further implicated Dr. Peebles as a Union man by conning him into putting his feelings down in letters which were published November 27, 1863, in the Houston Telegraph. Amidst the threat of mob violence, an appeal was made to the Texas Supreme Court, creating a conflict between Confederate military authority and states' rights. The appeal was successful on grounds of insufficient evidence and John Herndon, with John D. Newell, arranged to get the doctor out of Texas by way of the Union blockade ships. However, General E.K. Smith ordered the doctor rearrested before the escape was made. Dr. Peebles then spent some time in jail in Anderson. According to the doctor's son-in-law, P.S. Clarke, "Col. Herndon again used his influences and got permission to send him out which was done by way of Eagle Pass."

While Brazoria County had been the wealthiest county in the state before the war, total property values dropped from nearly seven million dollars in 1860 to less than three million dollars in 1866. Although John Herndon endeavored to recoup his prewar success, the economics of post-war Texas belonged to men like Abel H. (Shanghai) Pierce, who epitomized the best and the worst of the new breed. He also bought Herndon's Arabian horses. The Herndon Plantation was auctioned off and the town of Clute rose in its place. The Herndon family moved to Hempstead and later to Boerne where John H. Herndon died July 6, 1878.

6

Charles de Montel

Charles Scheidemontel was born in Konigsberg, Prussia, October 24, 1812. While he was a student at the University of Heidelberg, he belonged to a student military guard unit and may have received some naval training. Later he attended the Sorbonne at the University of Paris. Afterwards he emigrated to the United States, settling temporarily in Pennsylvania before setting out for Texas between 1836 and 1837. According to tradition, he arrived shortly after the San Jacinto Battle and joined Sam Houston"s army, serving as one of the men to guard General Santa Anna. According to this tradition, it was General Houston who suggested shortening Scheidemontel to de Montel.

The purchase of land in Palacios in 1837 provides the earliest verified date of Charles de Montel's arrival in Texas. By 1839, he had moved to San Antonio, taking up residence at the Lockmar Inn. He accepted a position as a Bexar County surveyor and became acquainted with another surveyor named John James.

Land was the major resource of the Republic of Texas and its soldiers were paid in land. Most of it was in the Bexar Territories, all the land west and north of San Antonio and mostly behind the Comanche Barrier. The Bexar County Surveyors were responsible for going out into this wild country to find and plot the individual tracts. They went out in heavily armed groups looking much like the Texas Rangers of the time, indeed, they were sometimes escorted by two or three rangers. Robert Hays, brother of Texas Ranger Jack Hays, was the chief Bexar County Surveyor. In 1848 John James took over that position.

The settlement of the West Texas Frontier and the movement of settlements beyond the Comanche Barrier began in 1844 with the Adelsverein and the Castro Colony. Henri Castro arrived in San Antonio in 1843 to find land for his impresario project. John James and Charles de Montel were on hand for any required surveying. When the first Castro Colonists arrived on the Texas coast the following year, Charles de Montel was there to meet them with ox wagons. He led these people and courted his future wife, Justine Pingenot, along the way to San Antonio. The rest of his life would be involved with the development of the areas that became Medina, Bandera, Uvalde, and Real counties.

While he continued as a surveyor, he established a ranch north of the new town of Castroville and engaged in the frontier Indian trade with Lipan Apaches who lived south of Castroville on Francisco Perez Creek and Tonkawas who were on Indian Creek to the north in the area that became Bandera County. On November 13, 1845, he married Justine Pingenot.

Henri Castro succeeded in settling around 2,000 people in the area that, in 1848, became Medina County. Charles de Montel was elected county clerk. That same year he also captained a ranger company stationed near D'Hanis. The following year the U.S. Army established Fort Lincoln at the ranger station and the ranger company disbanded.

In 1852, Charles de Montel joined John James and John Hunter Herndon in a partnership to develop the land in the upper Medina River Valley. James, Montel, & Company bought land in the area to add to what they already owned there, eventually amassing 15,000 acres. They plotted a town in a bend of the river south of Bandera Pass and called it Bandera City. Three families, the Saners, Milsteads, and Odems, moved from Boerne in 1853 to become the town's first settlers. Later that year some men from a shingle camp on the Guadalupe River, including Amasa Clark and O.B. Miles and his family, moved into town. Charles de Montel set up a horse-powered circular saw which provided employment for many of Bandera's first settlers.

In 1854, the Mormons of the Lyman Wight Colony moved into the region and set up camp a couple miles downstream from Bandera City. The Mormons found work in the construction of a water-powered mill for James, Montel, & Company. For a while it looked like they might become permanent settlers as some of them bought town lots and a school was built. However, Lipan Apache raids from Mexico that began that year, coupled with the already distressing Comanche raids coming through Bandera Pass, probably discouraged the Mormons. They moved 10 miles downstream, closer to Castroville, and founded Wight's Settlement which they called Mountain Valley, but in after years was remembered as the Mormon Camp. The community broke up after Lyman Wright's death in 1858 and many of its members settled in Bandera.

Eighteen fifty-four and 55 were dire years for Bandera City as many of the early settlers left the region due to the Indian raids. A promotional spot for "Bandera Valley and City" in the August 14, 1855 <u>San Antonio Herald</u> hedged, "Occasionally depredations occur from Indians, but settlers can come with safety and purchase and occupy this delightful country." Charles de Montel did what he could to counter the raids with a few chosen men. Governor Pease authorized James Callahan to raise a Texas Ranger company to patrol the area. Later the U.S. Army put some infantry soldiers in Bandera Pass and the following year a company of the 2nd U.S.

Cavalry established Camp Verde just north of the pass, increasing the prospects for the settlement of the region.

The Panna Maria settlement project had drawn many immigrants from the Silesian province of Polish Prussia, but there was not enough land available around Panna Maria for all the arrivals. In cooperation with Father Leopold Moczygemba, the polish colony's founder, Charles de Montel arranged for 16 Polish families in San Antonio to move to Bandera City. They arrived in the settlement February 3, 1855. Many of them took their first work in the new country in the completion of a mill race for the water-powered mill which had lain idle since the Mormons moved downstream.

Charles de Montel, who introduced cotton growing to Medina County, was a strong promoter of the Southern way of life. He owned nine slaves, including a man named Dave who tended the horses for the horse-powered mill in Bandera's early days. When the question of secession from the United States arose, Montel represented Medina County at the Texas Secession Convention where he served on the foreign relations committee. Later he served as provost marshal for Bandera and Medina counties.

In 1862, the Confederate State of Texas authorized a regiment of Texas Rangers to protect its frontier. Charles de Montel raised a company of 112 men mostly from Uvalde, Bandera, and Kerr counties. The company was organized at Camp Bandera before being divided between Camp Montel and Camp Verde. Captain Montel made his headquarters at Camp Verde. First Lieutenant Thomas P. McCall served as his quartermaster, while 2nd Lieutenant A.V. Gates was in charge of the troops at Camp Verde and Junior 2nd Lieutenant B.F. Patton was in charge of Camp Montel which was at Ranger Springs west of Bandera City. Lieutenant Patton's brother-in-law, John Sansom, stopped by Camp Montel after the Nueces Battle, according to the Frankie Davis Glenn biography of Sansom. A.J. Sowell accounts tell of other activities of the rangers. Sometime during 1862, according to one A.J. Sowell account, Captain Montel led a detachment of his company in coordination with detachments from other companies of the Frontier Regiment on a campaign to the Pecos River. They encountered overwhelming numbers of Comanches and narrowly escaped disaster before their return to the frontier forts from which they had begun. The company's monthly returns indicate that Captain Montel and some of his men were detached to Camp McCord (Frontier Regiment headquarters) for a time, but no other corroborating evidence has been found for the Sowell account. The references to "Captain Charles" on the muster rolls and monthly returns do seem to confirm the respect and affection the men had for their captain.

At the end of 1862, Charles de Montel helped reorganize the regiment in preparation for turning it over to the Confederate States Army, then made arrangements to take command of a commerce raider, the Confederate steamship Texas. His commission in the Confederate Navy is dated March 14, 1863. Congressman Wilcox, who arranged for the letters of marquis, wrote from Richmond March 22, 1863, "I hope your Letters will reach you safely & that you may get your Ship and play hell and destruction with Yankee commerce." Apparently, the Texas was sunk or damaged before Captain Montel could reach it. He spent some time doing administrative work for the CSA before returning to Medina County in March 1864, to raise a company for John Ford's Cavalry of the West. Twenty men were all he could muster. Two of them were 17 years old and another only 16. Big Foot Wallace, whose sudden departure from the region gave rise to rumors that he

Charles de Montel

had been killed by Indians, served as lieutenant of the company.

After the war Charles de Montel promoted the agricultural products of Medina and Bandera counties and continued his surveying work. In 1871 he formed the Charles de Montel Company to market his real estate and lumber interests. In the late 1870s, he lobbied to have the Southern Pacific Railroad built through Castroville. The effort failed when the railroad wanted money from the Castroville citizens which they refused to pay. To this day the railroad makes a wide berth around the town.

In 1881 Charles de Montel served as advisor to a Uvalde County minuteman ranger company that was known as the Montell Guards. He died the following year and is buried in the family plot on the ranch north of Castroville.

7

The Lymon Wight Colony

In the early 1840s, the leaders of the Church of Jesus Christ of the Latter Day Saints, the Mormons of Illinois, had begun to contemplate a move to some unsettled region where they could escape the animosity and mob violence of their neighbors. Among destinations being considered were Oregon, California, and Texas.

Meanwhile in Wisconsin Territory, the Black River Lumber Company provided construction materials for the temple that was going up along the Mississippi River in Nauvoo, Illinois, the Mormon capital. The leaders of the lumber mill settlement, Lyman Wight and George Miller, sent Texas-favoring proposals to Joseph Smith, the religion's founder. Lyman Wight's status as one of the Twelve Apostles of the Church gave his opinion considerable weight. March 1844, a special council of Mormon leaders sent Lucien Woodworth to Texas to investigate the possibilities of settling the frontier regions of the Republic. Woodworth presented a plan to President Sam Houston who agreed to forward the proposal to the Texas legislature.

Events overtook these preliminary feelers when Joseph Smith, the Mormon leader and a U.S. presidential candidate, was assassinated in June. Furthermore, the Republic of Texas became the state of Texas, nullifying the negotiations for land. Nevertheless, in the spring of 1845, Elder Lyman Wight set out for Texas with about 150 followers from the Black River Company. Among them were the Scottish families of Ballantyne, Chipman, and Hay.

Wight believed he was following the wishes of Joseph Smith and that the rest of the Mormon communities should be following him to Texas shortly. However, Brigham Young, the new Mormon leader, decided on the Great Basin area, the future state of Utah, as the main Mormon destination. Lyman Wight and his people settled and moved a number of times before reaching Bandera City. They spread water mill technology all across the Texas Frontier.

8

The Indian On The White Horse

The Bandera settlement began in 1853 when three families, the Saners, Milsteads, and Odems, arrived at the bend in the Medina River. The Rees family homesteaded a few miles away. Charles de Montel set up his horse-powered circular saw in the settlement and the prospect of jobs attracted some men who had been working shingles over on the Guadalupe River. Some of these men, like Amasa Clark, were single, but a few, like Orlando B. Miles, came with their families.

Although the region was considered one of the most dangerous in Texas at that time, the settlement initially went unmolested by Indian raids. This was at least partially due to the activities of the Indian agents who were busily negotiating settlement of the Texas Indian tribes onto reservations along the upper Brazos River. In the wider drama across the state, Indians faced the prospect of accepting reservation life or being considered hostile.

Major Robert Neighbors, Supervising Indian Agent in Texas, necessarily directed most of his attention to the Comanches. He succeeded in convincing the southernmost band, the Penatekas, to move onto the reservation. Many more Comanche bands were scattered across the plains above the Red River and their raids would continue into Texas and far into Mexico.

George Howard, a San Antonio merchant, politician, and ranger, was the subagent in charge of gathering the "border Indians," the small bands of Delawares, Tonkaways, and Lipan Apaches, who lived along the edge of the frontier settlements. They were all more or less in alliance with the settlements against the Comanches. The border Indians were to gather near Fort Inge at the headwaters of the Leona River where Reading W. Black lived and would soon establish the town of Encina (later called Uvalde).

In 1854 Frederick Law Olmsted and his brother passed by R.W. Black's house on their way to Mexico and observed "a portion of the tribe of Lipans, with a few Tonkaways, and Mescaleros—numbering, perhaps, in all, one hundred." Olmsted had hoped to meet a Lipan chief, but, "'Castro' was absent with some 'braves' on a visit to 'Chiquito,' the chief of another branch of the tribe now encamped in the Canon Uvalde." According to an A.J. Sowell account, another small group of Lipans was gathered near Fort Clark. A few other Lipan family or extended family groups were probably scattered all across the southwestern frontier, while some were already more or less settled in Mexico.

The Texas Delawares were near the end of their migrations from the Delaware River and went peacefully to the Brazos Reservation. Most Delawares were already established in the Indian Territory. The Tonkaway negotiations were complicated by an attack on their camp by a San Antonio mob intent upon getting their horses. The Tonkaways eventually moved to the reservation, but negotiations with the Lipan Apaches faired worse.

Lipans had fought Comanches for a couple hundred years and were loath to move to a reservation near their foremost enemy. According to Olmsted's account of the events of March-April 1854, Castro asked to stay along the border to make raids into Mexico. He offered to share the proceeds with the government. When this proposition was rejected, negotiations broke down and the Lipan bands began moving south of the border, mostly near San Fernando, Mexico. Their raids upon the

Texas Hill Country began in earnest and continued nearly 30 years.

In late February 1854, Elder Lyman Wight's "Mormon Colony" of Latter Day Saints, variously 150-250 men, women, and children, was meandering southwest from Burnet County. They were the millers, craftsmen, farmers, and stockmen, and their families who had left Illinois in 1845 expecting to be the vanguard of the Great Mormon Migration.

March 1, 1854, the main party of Elder Wight's followers pushed on to the south, crossing Bandera Pass. Some of the Mormon men were away chasing Comanche raiders who had stolen a number of horses the night before when the Mormons had camped on Verde Creek just north of the pass. The ox-drawn Mormon wagons rolled along while a herd of 100-200 head of cattle were driven nearby. Later that day they reached the shingle camp that had already been platted as Bandera City. One of the Elder's sons, Levi Lamoni Wight, celebrated his 18th birthday.

A few weeks later Lipan Apaches made the first Indian raid on the Bandera settlement: Oliver was a black man in bondage to Charles de Montel and in charge of eight to 10 mill horses. That morning when he went out to gather the horses, they were nowhere to be found. The Mormons, camped two miles downstream from the fledgling town, discovered many of their horses were gone, too. A group of men from both camps organized to go after the raiders.

Amasa Clark's version of this event is from his **Reminiscences of a Centenarian**, "told to and compiled by Cora Tope Clark" around 1929. The second version is from **Reminiscences and Civil War Letters of Levi Lamoni Wight** written in his own hand around 1909 and edited by Davis Bitton in 1970.

The Indian On The White Horse

[Amasa Clark]

As soon as it became known that the Indians had driven them off, Gideon Carter, Irvin Carter, O.B. Miles, Dan Turner, and several others took the trail and started up the river, and when they had gone several miles they met the horses coming back, as they had escaped from the Indians.

[Levi Lamoni Wight was among the "several others":]

We was soon on their trail and fowllowed them untill night fall and we could not follow in the dark with any certinty so we held to wait for day light. We had not more than got settled down for the [night] when it commenced raining and rained very hard [with] no let up till morning light apeared.

We resumed our chase, pushing with all the speed that our horses was able to stand, over mountains, through gulches, roiks, and brush. Late in the after noon, we sudenly met 6 of our horses that the Indians had captured makeing their way back. We rounded them up and took them along with us.

[Amasa Clark:]

Turner was left in charge of the horses and the other members of the party pushed on to overtake and chastise the Indians. Some distance further on they espied two Indians coming on the back trail with their heads down, following the horses' tracks. When the Indians saw the white men they dashed off and got into the brush.

[Lamoni Wight:]

[We] soon met 2 Indians in persuit of the horses. The Indians was within two hundred yards of [us] before we discovered each other. As soon as the[y] saw us they wheeled and put their horses to their best. We made hast[e] to persue them. A hot chase of 1 1/2 miles insud and they was forced to abanden their horses and take [to] the brush. We now had them behind us so their was no fears of them giveing the alarm to the other Indians. We had their horses and they were on foot so their was no fears of them to be dreaded in any way. In this chase I [was] so close to one of the Indians that as soon as he abandoned his horse I was in his saddle. As son as I got time to look at the horse I discovered that I was on my own horse. The exchange gave me no advantage in the way of a fresh horse.

[Amasa Clark:]

The white men went on and soon discovered the Indians' camp and made ready to charge it, but a deep gulch prevented them from advancing far, so they had to go around some distance to get to it. The Indians, seeing them approaching, left the camp and went up on a mountain, one of them riding a beautiful white horse, but during the charge which followed the Indian killed that white horse to keep him from falling into the hands of the white men.

[Lamoni Wight:]

But with out any delay we continued our persuit for about 8 milles and came in sight of the horses and Indans. They were at least 1/2 m[i]le away but in plain view. They evidently saw us and it was no use to take roundnce *[rounce: to be agitated]*. They disperd [with] no evedience of alarm. We was sure of a fight. We consulted a moment and the dission was to get to them as soon as posible. We charged down the long slope. The Indians moved slowly about, evedently geting ready for battle. One Indan in the time put saddle on horse and got on him. If boath parties had the long range rifels that is now in use

The Indian On The White Horse

some body might have got hurt, but their was none of these then in use.

On coming within about 100 yards of them, we sudenly came onto a deep ravine, imposible to cross on horse back. The Indans doughtles knew this and thaught that we would dismount and leave our horses, cross the hollow, and rush in to their camp, and while we were doing this that a portien of their force would keep up the fight untill the other portion got our horses and move off leaveng us a foot. Prehaps a portien of their force was allready behind us waiting to get the horses. But what or what not, we did not dismount but put our horses to their best [and] went up the hollow until we found a crossing.

When we rose the bank, the Indians were in full retreat. [They] went in to a brushey hollow and as we were in possion of every thing, camp, equipeg and all, we did not care to follow. They gave us a few shots however and the Indan that had put the saddle on [his] horse rode him up the side of the mountain a little way, killed his horse, and threw the saddle in to the brush. This might have ben the thought with them, that when we dismounted that he was to stampeed all the horses, our sadd[l]e horse and all, while those in camp was to engage us and make their escape in this brushey hollow spoken of. But whatever their plan of battle was, we got every thing they had except their saddles, and went home, leaveing the Indians to plan for another campain, which they no doubt completed before the next morning.

[Amasa Clark:]

The Indians made good their escape and the pursuers returned to the camp where they found a Bible and some boys' clothing in one of the wigwams. This occurred about twenty-five miles above Bandera.

These wigwams must have been among the last to be built by Indians in the Bandera region. Amasa Clark said the camp was at a site known as White Bluff and near the Medina River. The six horses that returned on their own may have been mill horses, their daily routine too deeply ingrained to depart from it for very long.

About this time, Lipan raids were reported at the Gallagher Ranch along San Geronimo Creek and the Forrester family's homestead on Helotes Creek. General Persifer Smith believed Mexican agents had influenced the Lipans. Robert Neighbors blamed George Howard. Whatever blame there was, the Lipan Apaches would not accept a reservation until there were only a handful of them left in the early 20th Century.

9

Contemporary Newspaper Articles

While John James was driving a herd of cattle to California in 1855, James, Montel & Company's Bandera City project got some much-needed promotional support from the San Antonio Herald:

Bandera Valley and City

> You ask my opinion of this country. I have seen [much?] of the early settlement of the justly [touted?] Bandera City and Valley. For desirable privileges for stock raising and general farming purposes, probably no section of country can exceed this. The City was founded under the direct patronage of our esteemed (though now absent) fellow citizen John James, and advocated and advanced by Charles de Montel, Esq. This desirable place of residence and adjacent valuable Country, must attract the attention of those wishing to purchase land for permanent residence in Texas; adapted as it is not only to the culture of grain, but more particularly to raising of sheep, hogs, and stock generally. Occasionally depredations occur from Indians, but settlers can come with safety and purchase and occupy this delightful country.

Among other newsmakers in the San Antonio Herald September 11, 1855 were Callahan's rangers and Charles de Montel:

Bandera City--More Indian Depredations

The Indians again paid this place a visit on the 3d inst., stealing three horses. Mr. C. de Montell, with two or three others, followed their trail three days, but did not succeed in overtaking them. On their return, were about thirty miles from home, they struck a fresh trail going west, which they took and were nearly up [with the] party when they met a small body of Rangers, who had met the Indians and killed one, (a Lipan,) and captured two horses and two mules branded with the Government Brand. The party saw three or four fresh trails going up the country, all with numbers of animals. The Indian killed was known to be a Lipan by Messrs. Montell, Luntzell and Hass.

One year ago, at Bandera City, there was a school with forty children, a thriving village, and situated as it is in a most healthy part of the country, bid fair to be a prosperous town. To Indian depredations alone is its decline owing. This, and other contiguous settlements, will have to be abandoned, unless some protection is afforded to the Settlers. A company at the head of the Hondo would protect all the lower settlements, as in almost every case the Indians come in by the head of the Hondo or Medina. We have no doubt as soon as practicable, Gen. Smith will give the matter his attention, and would recommend the settlers not to abandon their homes for a time at least.

10

The Mary Davis Petition

Bandarah Bexar Co. Sept. 21, '55

To E M Pease. Gov. Sir.

We the citizens of Bandarah would most respectfully call your attention to our exposed and dangerous condition.
 On Wednesday the 19, Ins't a party of thirteen Indians--armed with guns pistols bows & arrows attacked the family of Mr. R.N. Davis; and shot an arrow through the heart of his daughter Mary--(aged about 13 years): after having run about too yards she fell dead. His whole family would have been murdered had it not have been for the accidental coming up of a Mr. Stanford and Davidson. Mr Davis' daughter was brought down to this place yesterday evening & buried about 3 Oclock P.M.--There is a trail in different parts of this valley, which must have been made by some thirty Indians. We have ceased our work and are preparing to defend our lives and property in case we are attacked--which we have every reason to believe will be before this petition shall reach you--: but having no horses (having been robbed of every animal) we can not follow them or in any way avenge our wrongs. We are in a manner at their mercy--and if such mercy as the blood of Miss Mary Davis testifies to: Sir, there is too much of the blood of our citizens and of their children spilt in Bexar County by these merciless demons--to longer hesitate between peace and war. If we the citizens of the frontier have any right of protection from our Country, whether federal or State, in the name of God let us have it before it is forever too late.

Your fellow Citizen,

The Mary Davis Petition

J.P. Daniel	Lyman Wight
George Montague	Chr. Luntzel
R.H. Davis	Aaron Hurley
B. F. Bird	Charles Montel and Co.
L. W. Thornton	James Ballantyne
W. Ballantyne	G. M. Bird
M. Gillis	O. B. Miles
A. W. Stilwel	Samuel Calvert
John Mier	Andrew Hoffman
A. Smith	T. F. Carter
F. W. Davidson	Lyman Wight
C. c. Stanford	Meacham Curtis
T. E. Oborske	Levi L. Wight
Amasa Clark	John L. Gressmen
T. Kindla	Spenser Smith
G. Carter	Asher Grefsmen
George Hay	Jeremiah Curtis
Joseph Curtis	Frances Johnson
Richard Bird	

11

Wherever They May Be Found: Controversy and Consequences of The Callahan Raid, 1855

In 1855, the turmoil in Kansas and a Trans-Pecos expedition under Major John Simonson occupied most of the mounted troops who had been assigned to Texas. In their absence, raiding Indians harassed settlements all around San Antonio. Spread along the expanding frontier were Bandera City, Boerne, Comfort, the Ware and Patterson settlements, and Zanzenburg (Center Point). Smaller settlements included Sisterdale and Hodges Mill. Castroville, New Braunfels, San Marcos, and Fredericksburg were among the older frontier settlements by this time.

The Lipan Apaches raided from Mexico and from the Pecos and the Devil's rivers. Their main route passed between the headwaters of the Nueces and Llano rivers to the Frio Water Hole near the head of the Frio River. From there, various bands of raiders would fan out through the region that became Bandera County and into the settlements of the surrounding areas. Comanche raids continued to come mainly from the north, often filtering through Bandera Pass. Hondo Canyon provided outlet further south into Medina County. Raiders routinely came in on foot and left on horseback.

Governor E.M. Pease authorized a Texas Ranger company for the frontier even though no funds were available. July 5, he directed James Hughes Callahan, to raise the company. Captain Callahan was 40 years old and an experienced ranger. Engaged in a land venture with John D. Pitts and the Pittsburgh Land Company, he had just moved his family from Seguin to the new town of Pittsburgh which, in 1858, became known as Blanco City.

His instructions from Governor Pease stated, "It is expected that you will be actively engaged in ranging in their vicinity [basically the area north and west of San Antonio] unless it may become necessary to pursue any marauding parties of Indians that may be found in the neighborhood, in which case you are authorized to follow them up and chastise them wherever they may be found."

The company formed July 20 with 88 men, ages 16 to 44, mostly from areas around Seguin, San Marcos, and Austin. Eleven men were from the Hodges Mill area along Currys Creek, a tributary of the Guadalupe River. Among them were John William Sansom and Willis H. Jones. Valerius P. Sanders, a future sheriff of Bandera County, enrolled from Cibolo. Russell Varnell, a frontiersman from the Fort Inge area (near present-day Uvalde), served as a guide for the company.

In August, Captain Callahan made Bandera City his base camp. He rented one house to use as a commissary and another for a hospital. John Ridley was paid $26.25 for seven weeks' rent and $358.60 for supply and transport of 326 bushels of corn. Blacksmiths from Bandera, Kerr, and Gillespie counties readied the company's horses for service. Captain Callahan then sent a detachment to range through Medina County while two more detachments moved to forward camps in northern Gillespie County.

San Antonio newspaper accounts and the letters of William E. Jones detail some of the activities of these rangers. Jones, a former district judge, had a ranch near Currys Creek and a son in Callahan's Rangers. He kept in touch with his son and kept Governor Pease informed about events on the frontier.

The <u>San Antonio Herald</u> reported, "On the 30th [August], the Indians came to Mr. [John S.] Hodges place on Currey's Creek in daylight, and drove off about twenty head of horses. Mr. Hodges and his negro followed them, and as they crossed the Guadalupe, the negro shot one of them. Supposing themselves pursued, the Indians fled leaving nine head of horses." The article went on to say, "About the same time," a detachment of Callahan's Rangers "had a brush with the Indians, higher up on the Guadalupe." The rangers followed a trail until it ran cold then returned to the river to make camp. Two of the men went out and shot a bear which had disappeared when they came back with help to bring it into camp. They found a trail and followed it three miles before overtaking five Indians. The rangers charged immediately, killing one and severely wounding another. They recovered four horses, one mule, and a dead bear.

Judge Jones, writing to Governor Pease September 22, gave the site of this or another skirmish of August 30th as "thirty miles above the San Antonio and Fredericksburg Road—Two Indians were wounded and all their horses Six in number taken—Among other articles taken from this party was a shirt, apparently suited to a boy 12 or 14 years of age, with holes through as if made by a lance, or arrow." He noted further that on September 7, another detachment of rangers, "following a trail between the Guadalupe and Medina overtook a party of Indians—One was killed on the spot—one severely wounded and four horses taken."

All during this time Captain Callahan was formulating a secret plan: He would invade Mexico. His collaborations with slave owners who were negotiating with Mexican officials about the return of runaway slaves, encourages the suspicion that he may have had intentions of using his company to capture former slaves and Negro-Seminole Indians in Mexico. Whatever side issues may have been involved, he used the slaveholders' agent to lay the groundwork for a crossing that would be acceptable to Mexican authorities. At least that's what the captain thought had been arranged when he set out. His eventual association with William R. Henry made the venture seem to some contemporaries that this was just another filibuster attempt. Nevertheless, his primary intention was to attack Lipan Apache sanctuaries in Mexico. Historians still debate whether he had secondary or even tertiary objectives.

The second in command and quartermaster for the company, Lieutenant Edward Burleson, Jr., knew the captain's plan. The rest of the men were only aware that a big scout was in the works. The captain informed Lieutenant Burleson, August 15, "The Scout to start the 10 of september I intend to take all the men that want to go [.] And again August 31, "I wrote you Some time ago about arrangements as to our intended trip which I intend to carry out if possible [.] I believe some of the boys have found out the arrangement so I wrote to you as though my intention was to go to the upper country but that will I think be the best mode to keep the matter as much of secret as possible for I am bound to go to the Rio Grand if nothing happens more than I know of at present and you must try your best and have the provisions here as soon as possible for we cannot go until we get them and I want to be off by the 10 certain of it so that we possibl can[.]"

September 8, "in camp near Bandera," Lieutenant Burleson reported to Governor Pease that Sergeant Lewis and Corporal Taylor led their detachment in a fight against Indians, killing one and wounding others. They recovered some horses and mules that had been taken from the settlements. He stated further, "We [are] at this time waiting for ower provision and getting all the horses Shod So as we can take the biggest trail we can find and follow them up[.]" September 10 passed and September

12 Captain Callahan sent another letter to Burleson about the supplies. The lieutenant also had instructions to see about raising some more men in San Antonio.

Reading W. Black had recently set up a store at the head of the Leona River. The settlement that grew up there was called Encina and later Uvalde. Mr. Black noted in his diary September 15, "The rangers passed here [.] encamped 2 days [.] 130 of them on their way to Mexico [.]"

Lieutenant Burleson had spread the word about the need for more men. Nat Benton brought recruits from Seguin. William R. Henry, who had spent the summer trying to promote a filibustering expedition, brought recruits from San Antonio. Among the San Antonio men was Fabian Lucius Hicks, 27, just arrived in Texas from North Carolina.

At Encina the men formed two companies and elected new officers. Captain Callahan had one company of about 60 men and retained overall command. William Henry was elected captain of the other company, but some of the men objected to Henry's reputation. The matter was settled with Henry captain of about 35 men and Nat Benton captain of about the same number.

The Lipan Apache sanctuaries around San Fernando, Mexico, were well known in Texas. To stay within the letter of Governor Pease's directive, scouts were sent out to locate any recent Indian trails that could be followed into Mexico.

Lieutenant Burleson and about 20 men were left to hold the line in Gillespie County. He wrote a cryptic message to Governor Pease from San Antonio, September 15, "I, by order of Captain Callahan, take the liberty of addressing you a few lines, which will inform you that we have started a scout; that we intend to hunt up the Lipans in particular, and wherever we may find them."

The Callahan Raid, 1855

Callahan's Expedition reached Eagle Pass near Fort Duncan on the Rio Grande September 29. No opposition was expected from Mexican authorities in disarray from the recent revolt against President Santa Anna. Some of the men remained in Eagle Pass with a few sick men and the mule train, while 111-115 crossed into Mexico. On October 3, the rangers set out on the road to San Fernando. Later that morning, near Arroyo Escondido, the rangers clashed with a Mexican military force which had been alerted to the incursion. The force of several hundred included Indian auxiliaries. Callahan charged through them before taking up a defensive position in a ravine. In the charge, F.L. Hicks fired left and right with his double-barreled shotgun. During the race to the ravine, Nat Benton's son fell wounded. F.L. Hicks, Wesley Harris, and Hughes Tom emerged from the ravine under heavy fire to drag young Benton to safety. This desperate moment may have been when Private Hicks lost his six-shooter. Firing continued until early evening when the Mexican force, running short of ammunition, retired towards San Fernando. The rangers had four dead including Judge Jones' son, Willis. Seven rangers were seriously wounded and others had minor injuries. Mexican losses have been estimated at 30.

During the night Callahan led his men back towards the Rio Grande before camping outside Piedras Negras. Instead of re-crossing the river the next morning, he demanded and received the surrender of the town of about 2,000 inhabitants. The river was high at that time and difficult to cross with horses. Another reason for not re-crossing immediately seems to be that Callahan held a slim hope that reinforcements might arrive from San Antonio and he might continue his mission. Indeed, General Persifor Smith noted numbers of men coming into San Antonio as if on cue.

The town was held for a few days, but when confronted with the approach of Colonel Manuel Menchaca and 600-800 Mexican troops and Seminole allies, Captain Callahan, with about 90 men remaining in the town, ordered fire set to the outer houses of Piedras Negras to form a barrier that provided cover for the rangers' re-crossing. Another view, according to Seminole tradition, is that warriors shot flaming arrows onto the rooftops to drive the rangers from the town. A.J. Sowell's account states, "Hughes Tom, from Seguin, applied the first torch."

Captain Sidney Burbank, commanding Fort Duncan near Eagle Pass, only learned of Callahan's Raid after the rangers were in Mexico. Perplexed by a situation that could escalate into war and aggravated that Callahan did not re-cross immediately after Escondido, he nevertheless reported, "Under the circumstances I deemed it my duty to render assistance so far as it might be necessary to protect them while crossing, and I immediately placed several heavy guns in such a position as to command the ferry and crossing." Some of their horses had to be left behind, but most of the rangers were across by October 8.

Reading Black noted in his diary October 9, "heard from the Rio Grande that Pedras Negras was burnt to the ground." The following day "the Rangers got here and encamped for dinner." Fear of a Mexican retaliatory invasion nearly broke up the young town of Encina. Settlers left in a "general stampede." October 11, more rangers passed by and "Russ Varnell got home & reported Indians on the Nueses." Black's entry for October 27 states, "the bones of the volunteers were brought over from Mexico and intered on this side." As the rangers straggled into San Antonio, Judge W.E. Jones arranged hotel lodging for them.

In the meantime, the thin screen of rangers Callahan left to guard the frontier had proved inadequate. A tragic death occurred in the Bandera region shortly after Callahan's Rangers set out for Mexico. Amasa Clark recalled walking beside his freight wagon on September 19, going towards the shingle camps west of town when he met R.N. Davis carrying his daughter's body. Mary Davis was 13 years old and shot through the heart with an arrow. (Amasa Clark remembered her as Amanda.) The petition Bandera citizens sent to Governor Pease stated, "There is a trail in different parts of this valley, which must have been made by some thirty Indians. --: but having no horses (having been robbed of every animal) we can not follow them or in any way avenge our wrongs." Medina and other surrounding counties sent similar petitions to the governor.

General Smith had been promising protection to the Bandera region. By mid-October, he had more mounted troops available and Governor Pease disbanded the rangers in San Marcos. The following year saw a U.S. Army post, Camp Verde, established north of Bandera Pass.

Before the end of the year, the legislature passed an act to provide payment for the rangers. Ranger claims for loss of property took several years to sort out. F.L. Hicks submitted a claim for "one SixShooting Pistol lost in the Battle of Escondido" and loss of a "horse during the Engagement with the Enemy at Piedras Negras, Mexico on 7th October A.D. 1855." The diplomatic repercussions of the raid went on much longer.

Governor Pease retroactively supported Callahan, but admonished him that he ought not have burned Piedras Negras. James Callahan was killed in a quarrel with a neighbor in 1856. Callahan County is named after him. The Captain and his wife rest in the State Cemetery in Austin.

F.L. Hicks established a ranch west of Bandera City and, in 1857, married Hedwig Anderwald. He held various county offices over the years, including justice of the peace, sheriff, and hide and animal inspector. His Texas Ranger service continued with an enlistment in Montel's Company in 1862 and with county minuteman companies of the 1870s.

Mary Davis' burial was the first in Bandera City. Her name does not show up in the Bandera Cemetery Book and her grave may be among the unmarked.

Sources

"Bandera City--More Indian Depredations." The San Antonio Herald. September 11, 1855. Microfilm. Center For American Studies. UT Austin.

Burbank, Sidney, Captain. Report to the Assistant Adjutant General, San Antonio. October 11, 1855. Archives Division. Texas State Library. Austin.

Callahan, James H. Callahan to Burleson. August 15, 1855. Edward Burleson Jr Papers. Center For American Studies. UT Austin.

Callahan, James H. Callahan to Burleson. August 31, 1855. Edward Burleson Jr Papers. Center For American Studies. UT Austin.

Callahan, James H. Callahan to Pease. August 16, 1855. Edward Burleson Jr Papers. Center For American Studies. UT Austin.

Callahan, James H. Callahan/Burleson to Pease. September 8, 1855. Edward Burleson Jr Papers. Center For American Studies. UT Austin.

Callahan, James H. Special Orders Number 2. (Callahan to Burleson.) September 12, 1855. Archives Division. Texas State Library. Austin.

Callahan, James H. Special Order Number 6. (Callahan to Burleson.) September 12, 1855. Edward

Burleson Jr Papers. Center For American Studies. UT Austin.

Clark, Amasa Gleason. <u>Reminiscences of a Centenarian</u>. Naylor Company. San Antonio. 1930.

Denson, Mrs. Howard, Mrs. Billy Burnes, and Mrs. Howard Graves. <u>Bandera County Cemetery Book</u>. Bandera County Historical Survey Commission. Bandera. 197?

Ford, John Salmon. "Callahan's Expedition." <u>Plum Creek Alamac</u>. Volume 3 Number 2. (Fall 1985) Pages 10-11. [reprint of 1893 newspaper article]

Henry, William R. Statement Concerning Property Lost by F.L. Hicks. January 9, 1856. Records of the Adjutant General. Archives Division. Texas State Library. Austin.

Moore, Ike. <u>The Life and Diary of Reading W. Black: A History of Early Uvalde</u>. Arnold Graphics (for The El Progreso Memorial Library). Uvalde. 1997.

Muster Roll. Benton's Company. 1855. Archives Division. Texas State Library. Austin.

Muster Roll. Callahan's Company. 1855. Archives Division. Texas State Library. Austin.

Muster Roll. Henry's Company. 1855. Archives Division. Texas State Library. Austin.

Oates, Stephen B., ed. <u>Rip Ford's Texas</u>. University of Texas Press. Austin. 1963.

Olmsted, Frederick Law. <u>A Journey Through Texas: Or, a Saddle-Trip on the Southwestern Frontier</u>. Dix, Edwards and Company. New York. 1857.

Payment Receipts for Expenses Incurred by Callahan's Texas Ranger Company. 1855-56. Archives Division. Texas State Library. Austin.

Porter, Kenneth W. "The Seminole In Mexico, 1850-1861." The Hispanic American Historical Review. Volume 31. Number 1. (February 1951) Pages 1-36.

Report of Regional Indian Depredations. The San Antonio Ledger. September 8, 1855. Microfilm. Center For American Studies. UT Austin.

Shearer, Ernest C. "The Callahan Expedition, 1855." The Southwestern Historical Quarterly. Volume 54. Number 4. (April 1951) Pages 430-451.

Sowell, Andrew Jackson. Early Settlers and Indian Fighters of Southwest Texas: Facts Gathered From Survivors of Frontier Days. Ben C. Jones & Co. Austin. 1900.

Tyler, Ronnie C. "The Callahan Expedition of 1855: Indians or Negroes?" The Southwestern Historical Quarterly. Volume 70. Number 4. (April, 1967) Pages 575-585.

Tyler, Ron, et al, eds. The New Handbook of Texas. Texas State Historical Association. Austin. 1996. (http://www.tsha.utexas.edu/handbook/online/)

Wilkins, Frederick. Defending The Borders: The Texas Rangers 1848-1861. State House Press. Austin. 2001.

Winfrey, Dorman H. and James M. Day, eds. The Indian Papers of Texas and the Southwest: 1825-1916. Pimberton Press. Austin. 1966.

12

The Petition to Form Bandera County

[A description of Bexar County Precinct Number 18 appeared in the San Antonio Ledger July 13, 1854:]

Embracing all the Territory of Bexar County West of Precinct No. 19; North of Precinct 14; East and North of Precinct No. 13; and North of Medina County, and not included in Precinct No. 21.

[November 21, 1855 citizens of Precinct 18 of Bexar County requested the formation of Bandera County in this petition to Austin:]

To the Honorable, the Senate and House of Representatives of the State of Texas

We the undersigned Citizens of the County of Bexar, residing at the town of Bandera, Wights settlement on the Medina, and in the settlement on the upper Guadalupe [Zanzenburg? Comfort?] would most respectfully represent unto your Honorable bodies that we are residing at a distance of from forty to seventy miles from the City of San Antonio, the County Seat of Bexar County, that we frequently have legal Business to transact at the County Seat of our County and that when compelled to attend the inferior or District Courts of said County, either as suitors, jurors or witnesses, we are put to great trouble inconvenience and expense in consequence of the great distance from the places of our residence to the County Seat.

We further represent, that there is at present, a large number of permanent settlers living at the town of Bandera, on Bandera Creek, on the upper Medina, and on

The Petition To Form Bandera County

the upper Guadalupe: All of whom are desirous of having a new County established for their mutual convenience and advantage, and are ready and willing to erect suitable public Buildings as soon as said County is established.

We therefore in consideration of the foregoing pray your Honorable bodies to pass an Act creating said new County according to the metes and bounds of the Map or plot attached to this petition. We further pray that said County be named "Bandera County" and we pray lastly that the present town of Bandera be designated as the County Seat of Bandera County; as in duty bound we shall ever pray.

Wm Curtis	Simon Adamaez
FH Carter	Thomas Heuduk
Robert Ballantyne	Johann Pyka
William Ballantyne	F?W Oborsky
CC Standord	? Anderwald
Saml. W. Thomson	Frantz Anderwald
FW Davidson	Chs? Luntzel
Andrew Smith	Charles de Montel
M Gillis [Malcolm]	Wm Mylius
A Stillwell	TG? Calunna?
John Myre xxx	Albert Hyduki
Samuel Carr xxx	H. Adamicc
O.B. Miles xxx	Albt Adamice
A Hoffman [Andrew]	Aug. Klappenbach
Francz Jurecki	Joseph Knepik
Albert Haiduk	Amasa Clark
Johan Klugosz	F? Dlugosz?
P Martin [Paul]	Loammi L. Wight [Loammi Lemhi Wight]

F. Praussel?
Joforius? Grf? Wernett*
Joforius? Thalmann?
Lebreikt Thalmann
A? Nicolas?
Lyman Wight
James Ballantyne
Jeremiah Curtis
Bengaman F. Bird [Benjamin]
Lyman L. Wight [Lyman Lehi Wight]
M. Andrews
Gorg W. Bird [George]
Frances? Johnson
William W. Gaylord
Asher Grefsmen
Spenser Smith
John L. Frefsmen
Samuel Galbert
Sidney Gaylord
George Montague
C.O. Isham
Joseph Curtis
J.S. Southerland
Gubner Wm
Jn. Shneider
T??Ke? Frowador?

Meacham Curtis
Levi L. Wight [Levi Lamoni Wight]
Cecil Pingenot
Nicolas Pingenot
_____?
? Kalka
J. Kalka
Joforius? _____?
Kindla
W. Wallace
Henry Ruth
G. Daniel
x Daniels
J. Hamon
Fr? Kalka? or Kindla?
James Brown
Nicolas Frowador?
Daniel Turny
Gilb? x Guonz?
Gilb? z Frowador?
Martin? Dennis?
I? Adams?
Guonz? Mongold Jr?
Joforn? Frowador?
John Lalmoman? Or Thalman?

[* entry can be seen as two signatures making the total 88 or 89. The map mentioned is no longer attached. Nineteen new counties were formed in 1856. The "settlement on the Guadalupe" became part of Kerr County a week before the legislative committee got around to formalizing the boundaries for Bandera County.]

13

The First County Election Results

The State of Texas }
County of Bandera }

I the undersigned Commifsioner do hereby certify that at an Election held in and for said County on the 10. day of March A.D. 1856. by Virtue of an Act entitled "An Act to Create the County of Bandera."

That for the office of Chief Justice
O.B. Miles received —28 votes

For County Commifsioner
M. Curtis received —16 votes
Wm Curtis — 19 votes
Spencer Smith —16 votes
Wm. Ballantyne — 19 votes

For County Clerk
J.W. Poole received —17 votes
C.L. Short — 10 votes

For District Clerk
Augt. Klappenbach received — 22 votes

For Sheriff
A. Hoffmann - received — 16 votes
R.W. Davis — 11 votes

For Afsessor and Collector
F.F. Carter received —   19 votes
A. Hoffmann 9 votes

For County Treasurer
Gideon Carter received — 19 votes

The First County Election Results

For Justice of the Peace in Precint No. 1.
F.L. Hicks received —26 votes
H. Sloan —11 votes
F. Davidson — 15 votes

For Constable in Precinct No. 1.
F.C. Taylor received — 11 votes
A. Stilwell — 15 votes

For the Seat of Justice
Bandera City received — 28 votes

Given under my hand and Service for Seat at Bandera City this 21st day of March A.D. 1856.

Charles de Montel

Commifsioner appointed to organize Bandera County

[postscript]
No Election was held in precinct No. 2. on account of Indian depredations

14

U.S. Army Posts In The Bandera Region

After the U.S.-Mexican war ended, Brevet Major General William Jenkins Worth became departmental commander of Texas. Of 1,488 soldiers that gradually moved into the interior of Texas and out onto the frontier, most were infantry. Mounted troops, the army's dragoons or mounted rifles, made up only half a regiment. A line of forts went up along the San Antonio/El Paso road and along the frontier. General Worth stated the army's mission in General Orders Number 12: To protect lives and property, to prevent U.S. Indians from raiding in Mexico, and to protect non-hostile Indians. General Worth died in the James home on Commerce Street in San Antonio during a cholera epidemic. Brevet Brigadier General William S. Harney filled in until Brevet Major General George M. Brooke was assigned command of the department. General Brooke, in close cooperation with Texas governors, made extensive use of Texas Ranger companies as auxiliaries.

Brevet Major General Persifor F. Smith took over in 1851 and began work on a new line of forts beyond the frontier. The plan was to keep the mounted troops mostly near the settlements where forage for the horses could be purchased locally. The new forts were to be manned by infantry who would watch for Indian raiders and notify the cavalry posts when Indians were heading for the settlements. This passive and ineffective system was later modified to include mounted expeditions into the Indian strongholds north of the Red River.

Lipan Apache and Comanche raids harassed settlers in the new county of Medina in 1848. Until the army could get some mounted troops into the area, Captain Charles de Montel and Medina County rangers made their station two miles north of D'Hanis on Seco Creek.

Captain George A.H. Blake and Company A, 2nd Dragoons, were on the Medina River from December 1848 to April 1849. **Camp Florilla** was up river from Castroville. Quite likely it was named after Florilla Tyler. The officers of the 2nd Dragoons held the French-born wife of Lieutenant Charles H. Tyler of Company C in high esteem.

During January and February 1849, Captain Sidney Burbank and Companies A and B, 1st Infantry, set up **Camp Seco** two miles north of D'Hanis at the former ranger station. (When the Callahan Raid took place in 1855, Captain Burbank was in command of Fort Duncan on the Rio Grande.)

Lieutenant James Longstreet and Companies E and G, 8th Infantry, replaced the 1st Infantry companies in July 1849. Charles de Montel surveyed the site. As the post became established, it was named **Fort Lincoln** after Captain George Lincoln, 8th Infantry, who had been killed at the battle of Buena Vista in 1847.

Lieutenant Richard Dodge recalled a mounted patrol he led into the Guadalupe River Valley. He was riding a mule when he became separated from his men and was chased by Indians through Bandera Pass before safely reuniting with his patrol.

A Medina County settler, Edward Barnes, sold farm produce to the soldiers and became known as Potato Barnes. Later he moved up the Hondo Canyon into Bandera County.

The post was closed in 1852. H.J. Richarz, a Medina County rancher and, later, a Texas Ranger captain, made use of some of the buildings when he established his ranch headquarters there.

During 1855 most of the U.S. Army's Mounted Rifles in Texas were called away to Kansas, at the same time many troops were occupied with an expedition under Major John Simenson. Under these circumstances, Governor Elisha M. Pease authorized James H. Callahan to organize a Texas Ranger company for protection of the frontier between Medina and Gillespie counties. By 1856 the U.S. Army had more mounted troops available for service in Texas, including a new cavalry regiment. **Camp Davant** was a temporary camp on the south side of Bandera Pass in the summer of 1856. General Persifer Smith had been promising military protection to the Bandera region for some time.

At Camp Davant, Lieutenant John H. Edson commanded one company of Mounted Rifles. The namesake was 2nd Lieutenant William M. Davant who had drowned in the Rio Grande the previous year. In July 1856 work began on a permanent post on the north side of Bandera Pass.

Like Camp Davant, **Camp Stewart** was a temporary post during 1856. Captain John B. Magruder established the camp on Hondo Creek near the town of Quihi in Medina County. He had three companies of Mounted Rifles and a detachment of the 1st Artillery. Later Captain T.G. Rhett commanded one company of Mounted Rifles.

Camp Verde, a post with a two-fold mission, was located on Verde Creek north of Bandera Pass. For most of Texas history to that time, the pass had been considered one of the most dangerous locations in Texas. Comanche raiders from the north crossed through the pass to raid the settlements.

Jefferson Davis, the U.S. Secretary of War, created two new cavalry regiments and the beginning of a camel corps. The 2nd U.S. Cavalry would be posted in Texas. Company D would be responsible for Camp Verde's primary mission, frontier defense. An experiment with camels became the secondary mission of the post. In a time before the transcontinental railroad, their use might make communication with the Far West easier. Some U.S. military officers were impressed by the French Camel Corps then in use in Algeria.

July 8, 1856, Major Henry Wayne got the camels there and settled in before turning the post over to Captain Innis N. Palmer and Company D, 2nd Cavalry. Jose Policarpio (Polly) Rodriguez was the civilian guide (tracker) attached to the post. The camels, in separate operations, were sent on expeditions to explore the Big Bend area and made treks to California. They were often used to haul supplies from San Antonio to Camp Verde. The soldiers sometimes referred to their post as "Little Egypt."

General Smith had designated Polly Rodriguez as his headquarters guide around 1851. The men of Company D were lucky to get him as their guide in 1856. A guide needed a cool head, a good sense of direction, and knowledge of how to find water in unknown territory. Above all, he had to be able to follow a trail. Polly explained, "It takes a keen, smart man to trail; not many can do it. Experience is necessary. A trailer must not look along under his feet, but keep the trail far ahead of him, by signs he must notice, by broken twigs and weeds. A good trailer can ride at a gallop."

Company D did a lot of hard riding against Indian raiders during its several years at the post. A.J. Sowell and Polly Rodriguez gave accounts of the company's exploits. A unit citation can be found in the National Archives:

> January 28, 1858.—1st Sergeant W. McDonald, of company D, 2d cavalry, with fourteen men of that company, was sent out from Camp Verde, Texas,

to pursue and chastise some Indians who had been committing depredations on the San Jeronimo river [San Geronimo Creek]. After a rapid, but cautious, pursuit of four days he succeeded in surprising the party, and immediately charged upon them, killing two and recapturing the horses of which they had robbed the settlers. He had privates Stroacher and Hughes severely, and private Tanny slightly wounded. The sergeant speaks in commendation of hospital steward Arnold Stubb. Great praise is due to the guide, Polycarpio Rodrigues, for his untiring exertions and sagacity in the pursuit."

In 1857 Colonel Albert Sidney Johnston, commander of the 2nd Cavalry, set out from Camp Verde with an expedition to restore order in Utah. Johnston's Fork (or Creek) of the Guadalupe River is named from the route taken by these troops. (The name gradually changed to Johnson Creek or Fork after a family of Johnsons settled there.)

Colonel Johnston was temporary commander of the Department of Texas before Brevet Major General David E. Twiggs took over in March 1857. He was elderly and in poor health. He was sometimes on sick leave and other officers, including Robert E. Lee, often filled in for him. The department included 2,351 troops by this time.

For a while in 1858, a detachment of the 1st Artillery under Lieutenant W.M. Graham was at Camp Verde. This was the only time that the post had cannon. Also that year, Henry Ramsey became the civilian in charge of the camels.

In the summer of 1859, Captain Palmer and Company D went to other assignments. Polly Rodriguez was on a leave of absence to develop his Privilege Creek ranch, but had returned to Camp Verde by November. The new commander, Major Samuel P. Heintzelman, reorganized the post by placing Company A of the 1st Infantry at Camp Verde and by October had moved Lieutenant Wesley Owens and Company I, 2nd Cavalry, to a satellite post four miles north of Camp Verde on Turtle Creek. The new post was called **Camp Ives**, perhaps after Lieutenant Owens' West Point classmate, Lieutenant Bryton C. Ives, 1st Infantry, who had died at Fort Clark a couple of years earlier.

Camp Verde continued to provide economic stimulus to the area. Fodder for horses and camels was often procured locally. Major Heintzelman had his horse shod in Bandera City. On at least one occasion he took his wife shopping at the Klappenbach store. On another occasion they attended a revival meeting under a brush arbor in Bandera County.

The major wrote in his journal July 13, 1859, "Last evening there was a man brought me a note from Dr. Downs of Cottonwood Springs 8 miles beyond Bandera, that the Indians stole some mules & mares. Lt. Graham & 12 men left this morning in pursuit." August 25, 1859, "Some Indians rode through the streets of Bandera the other night. There is a party in pursuit but in such a manner that there is no prospect of their over taking them." November 9, "two citizens" delivered a letter from Judge E.F. Buckner to the major, which stated that, "A party of Indians killed two men 10 miles north of Quihi & drove off some horses. I sent 15 men in pursuit. Some Citizens are also out." The major noted further that, "The Indians are becoming so bold that it is dangerous to ride out alone." November 12, "I saw a S. Antonio paper. It is full of Indian depredations & murders."

The following day the major received orders to proceed to Brownsville with Camp Verde's Company A and nine other companies of cavalry, artillery, and infantry. The Cortina War on the Rio Grande was in full swing. Rip Ford and other Texas Rangers were involved in the affair. Lieutenant Owens was left in charge of Camp Verde.

When Lieutenant Colonel Robert E. Lee returned to Texas after subduing John Brown and his abolitionist raiders, he took Camp Verde's Company I, 2nd Cavalry, as his escort to the Rio Grande. Colonel Lee arrived at Ringgold Barracks March 31st, 1860. Major Heintzelman noted in his journal April 2, "I dined with him & after dinner he showed me his instructions. They are, if the Mexican authorities do not break up Cortinas & his bands for him to cross & do it. He will write to the Governor of Tamaulipas & ask him to put a stop to it." The Colonel's gentlemanly diplomacy ended the fracas for the time being.

Major Heintzelman returned to Camp Verde with the infantry company in late May. Company I continued service with Colonel Lee from March to October 1860. While Camp Verde's cavalry was in absence, Governor Sam Houston authorized Bandera County to form a minuteman Texas Ranger company. Tumlinson's Company of full-time Texas Rangers patrolled the region of the Sabinal Settlements for a couple of months.

James B. Cloud, a farmer from Tennessee, was a civilian guide at Camp Verde whenever Polly Rodriguez was not available. While Henry Ramsey was away, Cloud was also in charge of the camels. In an interesting side story, there was a free black woman, Helen Lacey, employed by the army at Camp Verde. The officers and their families enjoyed her company on social outings. Major Heintzelman's journal documents many social excursions from 1859 through 1860 in which she was included. July 2, 1860, in the early morning, the major's son, Charles, and the post doctor had gone over to the Medina River to fish. A group from the post rode out to join them: "Margaret & I with Mrs. Newton & Miss Helen Lacy rode on horse back." Others, including Captain James Caldwell, rode in an ambulance. They stayed on the river until seven that evening. "Polly our guide shot a buck & the Doctor caught a number of fish." Helen Lacey was among the guests at Major Heintzelman's 4th of July dinner. All this was too much for Cloud's Southern sensibilities. Later in July, he filed a complaint with local authorities. There was a law against free black people living in the state. The Kerr County sheriff arrived at the post with a warrant. The Camp Verde officers rallied to support Miss Lacey and found legal counsel for her. The hearing was put off until November. She was required to choose a temporary master until the proceedings determined her fate. Major Heintzelman made this entry in his journal November 14, "Capt. Caldwell went to Comfort this morning to attend to Aunt Lacey's case. The complaint Cloud made that she is a free cold. woman. Mary [the major's daughter] went with the Capt. & his children." Apparently, the issue was resolved in her favor due to her residence on Federal property.

As the Civil War approached, Major Heintzelman was called to Washington, DC. Major Carlos Waite took command of Camp Verde. The infantry company was sent elsewhere during this time. Major Waite called in Lieutenant Owens and the cavalry from Camp Ives and prepared for defense. His request for artillery was turned down, but February 4, 1861, received instead the return of Company A, 1st Infantry, to bolster his defenses.

Major Waite was promoted to colonel and command of the Department of Texas. He arrived in San Antonio February 18 to find that General Twiggs had just surrendered the department to the Confederacy.

The 2nd Cavalry left Camp Verde February 21 as Federal troops began to be evacuated from Texas. Camp Verde remained defiant until Lieutenant Hill and his infantry company surrendered April 1st.

As the Confederacy took over in Texas, Paul's Company was stationed at Camp Verde for two months. A succession of Confederate companies temporarily occupied the post after Paul's Company disbanded. The San Antonio Herald reported September 28, 1861, "Capt. Kampmann's fine company, consisting exclusively of San Antonio Germans, has been mustered into service. It has been sent to Camp Verde to relieve Capt. Buquor's company, which is ordered to the Rio Grande."

Early in 1862, an annex to Camp Verde became known as **Camp Prisontown.** Two miles southwest from Camp Verde, an estimated 600 Union POWs were held in Prison Canyon for several months. Captain Stoke Homes and a company of the 32nd Texas Cavalry (Wood's Regiment) guarded the Union prisoners. Andrew Jackson Potter, the Fighting Parson, was a private in the company. Jack Potter preached to the troops and on one occasion preached a sermon in Bandera. Measles broke out in this company and two men died. Confederate surgeon A.A. Shipp tended to the sick with Potter's help. Fearing Unionists would attempt to release the prisoners, the Confederacy moved them into more loyal territory until they were exchanged for Confederate prisoners.

During 1862 the state of Texas authorized a Texas Ranger regiment. Half of Montel's Company, Frontier Regiment, was based at Camp Verde, while the other half served at Camp Montel in Bandera County. A reorganization of the ranger force in 1863 resulted in Lawhon's Company, Mounted Regiment, until the state turned the regiment over to the Confederacy. May 1864, the Mounted Regiment became the 46th Texas Cavalry Regiment, C.S.A. Four companies, including Lawhon's, were sent to the Texas coast. Near the end of March 1865, 150 deserters and their spokesperson, Lieutenant Neel, left the coast. They gathered at Camp Verde asking the state government to place them back into the frontier service where they could protect their neighbors and relatives. Their fate in the last days of the Confederacy is unknown, but they probably just went home.

Federals troops began moving back into Texas in June 1865. That summer, a company camped on Bandera Creek near Bandera City. The army asked Polly Rodriguez to come back as guide, but he was too busy with his ranching, farming, and real estate interests. James Tafolla and William Ballantyne served successively as guides.

November 30, 1866, Camp Verde was reactivated as a U.S. Cavalry post. Three companies of the 4th Cavalry made the camp their base of operations. The following year, the post, commanded by Major J. S. Mason, was reduced to two cavalry companies. In 1868, the post was turned over to Captain H.A. Ellis and one company of the 35th Infantry.

The cavalry companies were sorely missed in the region. Sometime after they departed, March 25, 1868, J.B. Davenport presided over a meeting of Bandera citizens who petitioned the commander of the Military District to authorize the county to form a minute man Texas Ranger company. However, armed organizations were not allowed in the state during this period of Reconstruction.

The camels were sold in 1866, and the post closed in 1869. In 1870 the post became the ranger station for Captain John Sansom and Company C of the Frontier Force. The company included Theodore "Mico" Mimico, perhaps the only Arabian Texas Ranger in history.

Fort Roberts (or Camp Roberts?) became necessary when Colonel Ranald Mackenzie's 1873 raid into Mexico succeeded in subduing the Kickapoos who had been raiding the Bandera region, but inflamed the Lipan Apaches to more raids. Comanche raiders were still active as well. The Indian raids were of such intensity that year that Bandera County maintained a minuteman Texas Ranger company.

The army camp was home to a company of the 4th Cavalry for a short time. It has been remembered in the county as "The Old Soldiers' Camp" and in some traditions as "Fort Roberts." It was along the Sabinal River a couple of miles south of present-day Vanderpool. The camp consisted of a row of 12 rock chimneys 20 feet apart to which tents were attached. The chimneys were razed in the 1940s and the camp has all but disappeared from history.

Sources

Bechem, Robert. Letter to J.Y. Dashiell. May 13, 1862. Brigade Correspondence. Adjutant General Records. Archives Division. Texas State Library. Austin.

Boyd, Eva Jolene. Noble Brutes: Camels On The American Frontier. Republic of Texas Press. Plano. 1995.

Brown, John Henry. Letter to Pendleton Murrah. March 25, 1865. Governor's Records. Archives Division. Texas State Library. Austin.

Emmett, Chris. Texas Camel Tales. Naylor Printing Company. San Antonio. 1932.

Hunter, J. Marvin, ed. [From the Richard Irving Dodge memoir:] "Chased by Indians Through Bandera

Pass." <u>Frontier Times</u>. Volume 25. Number 7. (April 1948) Pages 169-173.

Hunter, J. Marvin. <u>100 Years In Bandera: 1853-1953</u>. The Bandera Bulletin. Bandera. 1953.

Minter, J.G., Major. Letter to Brigadier General Robert Beachem. May 10, 1862. Brigade Correspondence. Adjuntant General Records. Archives Division. Texas State Library. Austin.

Pierce, Michael D. <u>The Most Promising Young Officer: A Life of Ranald Slidell Mackenzie</u>. University of Oklahoma Press. Norman and London. 1993.

Rodriguez, Jose P. <u>Jose Policarpo Rodriguez: "The Old Guide</u>." Publishing House of the Methodist Episcopal Church, South. Nashville & Dallas. 1903.

Rodriguez, Rudi R., ed. <u>A Tejano Son of Texas: An Autobiography by Jose Policarpio "Polly" Rodriguez</u>. Texas Tejano.com. San Antonio. 2003.

Smith, David Paul. <u>Frontier Defense In The Civil War: Texas' Rangers And Rebels</u>. Texas A&M University Press. College Station. 1992.

Smith, Thomas T. <u>The Old Army In Texas: A Research Guide to the U.S. Army in Nineteenth-Century Texas</u>. Texas State Historical Association. Austin. 1999.

Sowell, A.J. <u>Early Settlers and Indian Fighters of Southwest Texas: Facts Gathered From Survivors of Frontier Days</u>. Ben C. Jones & Co. Austin. 1900.

The Texas Historical Records Survey. <u>Inventory of the County Archives: No. 10 Bandera County</u>. WPA. San Antonio. 1940.

Thompson, Jerry, ed. Fifty Miles and a Fight: Major Samuel Peter Heintzelman's Journal of Texas and the Cortina War. Texas State Historical Association. Austin. 1998.

Tyler, Ron, et al, eds. The New Handbook of Texas. Texas State Historical Society. Austin. 1996. (Online).

Walton, Greg, ed. Bear Meat 'n' Honey: An Oral History of the Sabinal Canyon. Acorn Press. Austin. 1990.

15

Jose Policarpio Rodriguez

A cone-shaped hill near Privilege Creek and visible from Highway 16 just east of Bandera is known as Polly's Peak. While initially named after J.B. Polley, a surveyor and brother-in-law of John James, the hill has always been associated with Jose Policarpio (Polly) Rodriguez whose ranch lay in its shadow. The Old Guide was born in 1826, in Zaragoza, Mexico.

In 1841, his father moved the family ranching operations to the San Antonio area. Young Polly studied the gunsmith trade as an apprentice, but was more interested in hunting. While hunting was great sport for the teenager, it was also a business, for the meat could be sold in San Antonio. By 1847 his hunting excursions, sometimes with his friend, Jacob Lynn, extended as far from San Antonio as the eastern part of what is now Bandera County. He went well-equipped with an ox-wagon, hunting dogs, extra horses, and plenty of fire-arms. One trip yielded nine bears, three panthers, twelve turkeys, and assorted small game. On another hunt he recalled, "We killed several deer, a number of turkeys, one bear, and cut several bee trees. We found a bunch of wild cattle, most of them black or brown. We got after one and killed her."

The Bexar County surveyors were busy finding all the tracts of land with which the Republic of Texas paid its soldiers. Polly Rodriguez joined some of the surveying parties that went into the vast Bexar Territories, all the land west and north of San Antonio. In 1849, he signed on with the Whiting Expedition, which surveyed a route from San Antonio to El Paso. His knowledge and skill in the outdoors greatly impressed the U.S. Army officer in charge, Lieutenant William Whiting, who made this notation in his journal:

> This boy Policarpo is one of the most valuable members of my party—a patient and untiring hunter, an unerring trailer, with all the instinct and woodcraft of the Indian combined with the practical part of surveying which he has learned from Howard; moreover, a capital hand with the mules. I don't know of any person whom I would rather have in the woods.

Lieutenant Whiting went on to other duties after the expedition, but recommended the young frontiersman to the army brass in Texas. A similar expedition under Colonel Joseph E. Johnston further extended Polly's reputation as a frontiersman. Interviewed shortly thereafter by General Persifer Smith, Polly became the general's headquarters guide. In the following years he served with the army all around the San Antonio area, out to El Paso, and down to the Texas coast.

In 1852, he married Nicolasa Arocha whom he used to see in San Antonio when he returned from his hunting trips as he said, "One day I was returning from a hunt, and I saw her and another on the walls of the old Alamo building. They called to me to know where I had been, and asked me to come up to them."

On one occasion, near El Paso, he was sent into Mexico to track some deserters. On his return he met a recently discharged war veteran named Amasa Clark. Clark was with "Coon's Train" which brought supplies from San Antonio to the army posts around El Paso. Within a few years both men would be living in the area that became Bandera County.

October 3, 1854, he was the guide for Captain John G. Walker with Companies D and K, Mounted

Rifles, when they took up the trail of Lipan Apache raiders who had stolen cattle near Eagle Spring along the El Paso/San Antonio Road. The Mounted Rifles came upon the Lipan camp and attacked. Army documents reveal that one soldier was killed while Lieutenant Eugene A. Carr and Polly Rodriguez were wounded. Seven Indians were killed.

In 1856, he was on assignment with Captain J.G. Walker and a company of Mounted Rifles at a river crossing used by raiding Indians about 50 miles southeast of San Antonio at the junction of Conquista Creek and the San Antonio River. He came down with a fever or, as he put it, "I contracted chills at Conquista Crossing, and was ordered to go to Camp Verde with Captain Palmore, of the Second Cavalry." The 2nd Cavalry was a new regiment, the first to be trained in the light cavalry tactics needed to compete with Indians. Major Henry C. Wayne oversaw the layout of Camp Verde and got the camels settled in before turning over command of the camp to Captain I.N. Palmer and Company D.

The camels were an experiment in supply and communication. They were trekked back and forth between Camp Verde and various forts all along the way to California. They were sometimes used as pack animals for cavalry patrols or to haul supplies from San Antonio. On one occasion in 1857, they wandered away from the camp and Polly Rodriguez was given a detachment of cavalrymen and told to go find the camels. He tracked them from Bandera Pass to Bandera and then east along the Medina River to the mouth of Privilege Creek where the camels had wandered upstream. He was so impressed with the land and game (he shot a bear or two) around the creek that at his next opportunity, he found who owned the land (John James) and bought 360 acres. He had some problems with the title as he recalled:

I could not get a title to my land until after nine years of delay and trouble. The State authorities refused to make a title, as it was not surveyed according to regulations. But by dividing it up and changing the survey, Mr. James finally got me the title.

Eighteen fifty-seven and 58 were busy years for Polly Rodriguez and the 2nd Cavalry. His abilities as a tracker and frontiersman were put to severe test. He tracked Indian raiders for days at a time. Sometimes the army would loan his services to the various minuteman ranger companies that were raised around the region.

His generosity was well-known. After a successful pursuit of Indian raiders in 1857 Rodriguez brought a few trophies back to Camp Verde: A shield and a panther-skin quiver were given to an officer who pleaded to have them. A scalp was already spoken for, or so he thought:

> I had scalped the dead Indian before we left him the evening before, because a lady at Camp Verde said to me as I was leaving: "Polly, bring me a scalp."
>
> I took it to her, but she would not have it. She said in a very frightened voice: "I don't want it. I didn't think you would kill an Indian."

Another 1857 pursuit related in Polly's autobiography resulted in two soldiers wounded during a skirmish with the Indians. This seems to be the firefight reported in army documents as taking place February 13, 1857 when a detachment of Company D under 1st Sergeant Walter McDonald caught up with Comanche raiders on Kickapoo Creek near the head of the South Concho River. Dr. James Nowlin was with the troopers on this occasion, but he could only apply first aid to the wounded soldiers in the field. One of the soldiers was seriously wounded and the nearest surgical facility was at Fort McKavett. Polly Rodriguez had never been there, but he knew the direction and the direction of the wind. He led the detachment straight to the fort, traveling mostly through the night. In later years, he talked about tracking:

> It takes a keen, smart man to trail; not many can do it. Experience is necessary. A trailer must not look along under his feet, but keep the trail far ahead of him; by signs he must notice, by broken twigs and weeds. A good trailer can ride at a gallop. I have trailed where every other man said there was no sign, and would not believe I was on the trail until we came upon the Indians. The Indian is very smart to cover up his trail, I don't know anybody that can equal him.

January 28, 1858 he led Sergeant McDonald and a detachment of Company D to Comanche raiders who had reached the South Llano River. Stolen horses were recovered after a skirmish in which three soldiers were wounded and two Indians killed. A Unit Citation can be found in the National Archives commemorating this action:

> 1st Sergeant W. McDonald, of company D, 2d cavalry, with fourteen men of that company, was sent out from Camp Verde, Texas, to pursue and chastise some Indians who had been committing depredations on the San Jeronimo river [San Geronimo Creek]. After a rapid, but cautious, pursuit of four days he succeeded in surprising the party, and immediately charged upon them, killing two and recapturing the horses of which they had robbed the settlers. He had privates Stroacher and

Hughes severely, and private Tanny slightly wounded. The sergeant speaks in commendation of hospital steward Arnold Stubb. Great praise is due to the guide, Polycarpio Rodrigues, for his untiring exertions and sagacity in the pursuit.

Polly and Nicolasa Rodriguez lived at Camp Verde while a caretaker family lived in their Priviledge Creek ranch cabin. In 1859, the captain gave permission for Polly to live at the ranch as long as he remained on-call. He built a sturdy two-story stone house. At the same time, he invested in real estate in the area and sold parcels of land to settlers. A small community grew up around the house that served as a fort in times of Indian raids.

While Polly was busy developing his ranch and real estate interests, a new commander, Major S.P. Heintzelman, took over at Camp Verde. Company D had been replaced by an infantry company while Company I of the 2nd Cavalry was stationed at nearby satellite post, Camp Ives (on Turtle Creek). When Polly finally returned to the camp for steady duty November 1, 1859, he was the "new" guide to Major Heintzelman:

> Polly our new guide came & reported three Indians stole his horse 14 miles from here. I sent 15 men with him in pursuit. He thinks he can overtake them & that there is a large camp on the headwaters of the Concho.

Polly resumed the routine of tracking and pursuit. December 14, 1859, he led Corporal Patrick Collins and a detachment of Company I on the trail of Comanche raiders and came upon them dismounted in camp near the north branch of the Guadalupe River. In the subsequent firefight, one Indian was killed and three wounded. Fifteen horses were recovered.

However, life was beginning to change for Polly Rodriguez. He had developed an interest in gardening during his absence from Camp Verde. Besides honey from bee trees and meat from wild game, his garden produce often graced the soldiers' tables.

Major Heintzelman's journal documents the off-hours activities on a frontier army post. Polly Rodriguez went on hunting and/or fishing trips with the major and other officers and accompanied them and their wives on leisurely rides through the countryside. Major Heintzelman wrote in his journal September 22, 1860:

> We—Margaret & I & Dr. Byrne, Mr. Newton, Pollycarp & Miss Lacy rode out in the hills about six miles & cut a bee tree & spent the day. We brought home two pails of honey & spent a very pleasant day. All were pretty tired.

> October 1, 1860:

> Dr. Byrne & Mr. Pollycarpio spent the evening on our stoop. To-day has been quite warm. I have been trying to read.

> December 7, 1860:

> I went with Dr. Byrnes, Mr. Newton, Policarpo the guide & Francisco on a bear hunt. We were gone 8 hours & in the saddle 7 ½. We saw one bear & cub but the dogs were off & they escaped. The country is very rough & difficult. We saw two deer & three turkeys. The weather delightful.

With the approach of the Civil War, Major Heintzelman was called to Washington, D.C. Major Carlos A. Waite assumed command of Camp Verde and began making preparations for its defense. He soon received a promotion to colonel and was about to take command of the Department of Texas from the retiring General

David Twiggs, when General Twiggs surrendered to Secessionist volunteers in San Antonio February 18, 1861, ending the hope of some Federals of keeping a Union foothold in Texas. Polly Rodriguez remembered the times:

> The United States troops left Camp Verde and the State, and we passed under Confederate authority. It was a sad day for me when I had to part from the United States troops. I had been with them for twelve years, and I had seen much hard service with them, and had many good friends among them. Major Wait was in command, and asked me to go away with them, but I could not. It would have been to leave everything behind, and really forsake my family and home.
>
> The Confederate authorities at San Antonio secured for me a commission as captain in that service and sent for me and offered it to me. But I declined. My heart was really with the United States, that I had served so long.
>
> They accused me of being a Union man. I said: "Now, it is like this: If I were out with ten men and nine should decide against me, I would be compelled to accept their decision. The State has seceded, and I accept the situation; but if I could have had my way, it would not have done so."
>
> So I went back to my home and joined the "Home Guards." We elected one of my neighbors, a Mr. Mitchell, captain.

Bladen Mitchell, whose horse ranch was along the Medina River at Mitchell's Crossing, ten miles from Bandera City, was elected captain of the company March 30, 1862. Polly served as a private and had this recollection:

It was our business to defend the neighborhood from the wild Indians and to keep down the disorderly element at home. I served four years, the whole period of the war, in this company. We were almost constantly on the scout, and had many unimportant encounters with the Indians.

The company was supposed to be run by strict army regulations, but in practice the frontier settlers had little use for such things. When Polly asked the captain for leave to escort his sister on a visit to relatives in Mexico, he said sure, go ahead. On the return trip, dressed in "a fine buckskin suit [bought] over in Mexico, and a fine Mexican Hat, beautifully fixed up in Mexican style," he stopped by a gambling saloon in San Antonio where he was accosted by a provost marshal who asked to see his written pass. For a few tense moments there was the threat of jail or a shoot-out, but a family friend, Antonio Manchaca, stepped in and vouched for him.

When the war ended our company of home guards was disbanded, and in a few months the United States troops returned. They had heard of me, and the company that was camped on Bandera Creek near the town sent for me and offered me a hundred dollars a month to join them and act as guide and escort. I could not accept the offer, as I had so enlarged my place and had so many interests on my hands—stock of all kinds—and was making money trading.

S.P. Heintzelman returned to the region for a visit and stayed at Dr. Charles Ganahl's ranch along the Guadalupe River. He made this entry in his journal October 11, 1866, "Policarpo Rodriguez arrived here before breakfast. Mrs. Ganahl sent Mr. Newton's note to him & he came all night." The old friends had a good reunion with much hunting and fishing and a visit to Polly's ranch. General Heintzelman noted in his journal that Policarpo was setting out an orchard and flowers on his cattle rancho. The visit ended a few days later as the general wrote, "Polly is one of the best Mexicans I ever met with & I parted from him with regret."

The cattle business picked up as new markets for Texas cattle began to open. By 1868 the Bandera region was bustling with activity as Leopold Haby remembered his first open-range roundup beginning at the ranch of August and Celeste Pingenot in Bandera County, "August Pingenot joined the party and they hunted and rounded up cattle throughout the country around Bandera, penning at the ranch of Polly Rodriguez, at the Jack ranch, at the Bandy ranch, and at Bladen Mitchell's."

The Polly Settlement increased from a few families to more than 10 through the 1870s. The threat of Indian raids and outlaws gradually diminished on the frontier and civilizing influences began to be felt. Polly's cousin, James Tafolla, started a self-improvement society for the men of the community. Rodriguez explained, "When he settled down after the war he was elected [constable] and although, like the rest of us, he had been pretty wild, he wanted to do better as an officer." They had Bible readings, debates, and discussions.

Polly Rodriguez served the public as a justice of the peace in 1864 and was elected to another JP term in 1870. In 1866, he was among Bandera's county commissioners. Blas Loya, James Hill, and he were the first trustees for the Polly public school that opened in 1881. He donated land for the school and, after joining the Methodist Church, built a chapel where he sometimes gave sermons.

In 1885 Francisco Gerodetti, an Italian immigrant, bought land for a ranch from Polly Rodriguez and set up a general store in Polly. The Polly post office was closed after Gerodetti died in 1911.

In his later years, Polly Rodriguez was a fervent evangelist, a rancher and gardener who took great pride in his prizes from the San Antonio agricultural fairs, as well as a proud family man. His first wife, Nicolasa, who bore him five children, died some years before he remarried to Anastacia Salinas in 1903. Four more children were born to the family before Policarpio Rodriguez died while in Poteet, March 22, 1914.

Sources

Bechem, Robert, Brigadier General, TST. Report to J.Y. Dashiell. April 10, 1862. Brigade Correspondence. Adjutant General Records. Archives Division. Texas State Library. Austin.

Boyd, Eva Jolene. Noble Brutes: Camels On The American Frontier. Republic of Texas Press. Plano. 1995.

Edwards, Jay. "A History of the Privilege Community." The Bandera County Historian. Volume 9. Number 2. (Summer 1986) Pages 1-3.

Hunter, J. Marvin. 100 Years In Bandera: 1853-1953. The Bandera Bulletin. Bandera. 1953.

Hunter, J. Marvin. The Trail Drivers of Texas. Cokebury Press. Nashville. 1925.

Jennings, Frank W. "A Man Called Polly: Texas Pioneer Lived a Life of Adventure." The San Antonio Express-News. August 18, 1991. San Antonio.

McDaniel, Niki Frances. "A Man Called Polly: Descendant Helps Keep Legend Alive." The San Antonio Express-News. August 18, 1991. San Antonio.

Muster Roll. Mitchell's Company (The Bandera Home Guardes). Frontier Organization. Texas State Troops. February 6, 1864. Archives Division. Texas State Library. Austin.

Rodriguez, Jose Policarpo (as told to Rev. D.W. Carter, D.D.) <u>Jose Policarpo Rodriguez: "The Old Guide:" Surveyor, Scout, Hunter, Indian Fighter, Ranchman, Preacher: His Life in His Own Words</u>. Publishing House of the Methodist Episcopal Church, South. Nashville and Dallas. 1898?

Rodriguez, Rudi, ed. <u>A Tejano Son of Texas: An Autobiography by Jose Policarpio Rodriguez</u>. Texas Tejano.com. San Antonio. 2002.

Smith, Thomas T. <u>The Old Army In Texas: A Research Guide to the U.S. Army in Nineteenth-Century Texas</u>. Texas State Historical Association. Austin. 2000.

Thompson, Jerry, ed. <u>Fifty Miles and a Fight: Major Samuel Peter Heintzelman's Journal of Texas & the Cortina War</u>. Texas State Historical Association. Austin. 1998.

Tyler, Ron, et al, eds. <u>The New Handbook of Texas</u>. Texas State Historical Association. Austin. 1996.

16

Keeping The Camels:
The Camel-handlers of Camp Verde

When the U.S.S. <u>Supply</u> returned from the Middle East with the camels in 1856, 9-12 camel handlers and saddle-makers were also on board. They had signed with the U.S. Army as civilian employees for one year. Among them with their acquired nicknames were Hadji Ali (Hi Jolly), Teodoro Mimico (Mico), George Caralambo (Greek George), Hagiatis Yannaco (Long Tom), Anastasio Coralli (Short Tom), Elias, Kostes, Alexandrino, and Georgino. The "Turks," as they were called, were mostly Greeks and Syrians who had been living around Smyrna, Turkey, and other locations in the Ottoman Empire. Major Henry Wayne oversaw their overland trek from Indianola to Camp Verde before turning the post over to Captain I.N. Palmer. The post had been established in 1856 for a company of the 2nd U.S. Cavalry, but doubled as the easternmost station of Secretary of War Jefferson Davis' camel experiment.

 The Middle Eastern camel handlers and saddle-makers finished their contracts, but there was a long delay in their pay. July 1857, Captain Palmer paid them with $1,100 from his own funds. Most of these men returned to the Middle East, but a few of them stayed. Hadji Ali had come to find gold. He left with George Caralambo for California. Hi Jolly's search for gold achieved legendary status in Arizona. Elias eventually settled in Mexico. Hagiatis Yannaco was around Camp Verde until about 1869 when he joined a traveling circus. Theodore Mimico remained at Camp Verde for many years and lived in Bandera County after the Civil War.

Theodore "Mico" Mimico was born Mimico Teodora in Turkish Smyrna in today's country of Syria. In 1870, he served in Captain John Sansom's Company of the Frontier Force of Texas Rangers. A petition of Kerr (?) County citizens attests to his popularity in the area. When he was sentenced to prison after accidentally killing a man in a scuffle, the petition secured him a governor's pardon. Mico Creek in Kerr County is named after the him. He died in 1896 and is buried in Bandera County.

A civilian employee, Henry Ramsey, took charge of the camels in 1858, but seems to have been absent, probably on expeditions with the camels, for much of 1859-60. James Cloud, a post guide, managed the camels when Ramsey was away. Another civilian, Amasa Clark, recently married in 1859, took a job as a camel herder for about a year. He collected camel hair during that time and soon had enough for a mattress and two pillows. At least one of the pillows has survived in the Frontier Times Museum in Bandera.

Major Heintzelman, Captain Palmer's successor, noted in his journal that an expedition was about to get under way May 31, 1860, "In the afternoon Mr. Ramsay got back, with the news that the Alamo was burned. That portion across the street from the main building, with old wagons, wheels, hay & materials. The loss to the government 30 or 40 thousand dollars. Mr. Edgar also came with him—for the camels. They take 20." Lieutenant William H. Echols, on his second expedition to the Trans-Pecos, set out from San Antonio June 11, with 20 camels and their handlers. Lieutenant Holman and 20 infantrymen provided the escort.

Chris Emmett recorded the words of David N. Wharton who remembered Mico Mimico and the dances that were sometimes held at Camp Verde during the (early part of the?) Civil War:

> Oft-times because of the great distances to the homes of the dancers, everybody would spend the night at the old fort, and then Mico, who had unprotestingly gone over to the Confederates, would bring out Old Major, the remaining Bactrian. Mico would hold his head whilst the ladies would mount him for a ride around the parade-grounds.

Camp Verde and the camels, formerly U.S. property, now belonged to the C.S.A., but their care was administered by the state of Texas. Camp Verde therefore fell under the authority of Brigadier General Robert Bechem commanding the 31st Brigade, Texas State Troops, headquartered at New Braunfels. Henry Ramsey, a Bandera County resident after the war, had been at Camp Verde since 1858 and was overseer for the camels during most of the war. During April and May 1862, he traveled to New Braunfels and San Antonio attempting to get exemption from military service for himself and his four employees while the state and Confederate military authorities sorted out who had the authority to grant that.

Office of Chf Ordn Dept Texas
San Antonio, Texas

May 10/62

Sir

I have the honor to request that the overseer and four herders in charge of the Camels belonging to the C. States and now at Camp Verde Texas may be excused from malitia drill as their duties are constantly required in the public service herding, and taking charge of the Camels.

> Very Respectfully
>
> Your ObtSvt
> J.G. Minter
> Major CSA
> notation illegible]

> Brig Genl Rrtt Becham
> 31st Brigade T.S. Troops
> New Braunfels
> Texas

From the representation which Mr. Henry Ramsey, the overseer at Camp Verde has verbally made to me about his situation, and that of the herders for whom excemption from military duty is claimed, namely besides himself for Candelano Treninio
  " Ephetasio Flores
  " Thre. Mimico
& " J. Tiffoje, I cannot but advocate the request of Major Minter, and wish the exemption would be granted.

> New Braunfels May 13th 1862
> Robert Bechem
> Brig. Genl. 31st Brigade T.S.T.
> [Adjutant General clerical notation:]
> Received & Spec. Orders issued
> May 15, 1862

In June 1862, General Hamilton Bee appointed new provost marshals for Texas counties. Charles de Montel, captain of a company in the Frontier Regiment, was named provost marshal for Uvalde, Medina, and Bandera counties. James M. Starkey was provost marshal for Kerr

County and made a list of the names, ages, and occupations of the county's men, including the men who kept the camels at Camp Verde:

> 48. Epitacio Flores — Govt. Employee — 31
> 49. Theodore Minacio — Govt. Employee — 30
> 50. Candelario Trevino — Govt. Employee — 35
> 51. J. Tafolla — Govt. Employee — 25
> 52. Henry Ramsey —Govt. Employee — 31

James Tafolla had served as a bugler in the 2nd U.S. Cavalry at Camp Verde before the war. He was a Bandera County constable after the war and formed a self-improvement society in the Polly Community. Polly Rodriguez, a Mason, helped in the organization. He recalled his cousin's actions in an 1857 fight between a unit of the 2nd Cavalry and Comanches:

> The bugler, Jim Tafolla, saw the Indians after our horses, and started to meet them. I called to him that he would get killed, but he went galloping right after those two Indians, shooting at them with his pistol. The Indian in front had a shield on his arm, and I could see when the bullets hit the shield that they knocked up the dust close around him as they glanced off. These shields are made of several thicknesses of rawhide, and get so tough and hard that unless a bullet strikes them very square and solid it will glance off. Tafolla kept advancing and shooting. The Indian kept his shield whirling from side to side, and the bullets glanced off. When close up, Tafolla's pistol refused to fire; a cap had caught, and the cylinder would not revolve. The Indian shot with his bow and Tafolla struck at his head with his pistol. The Indian dodged down and escaped. Tafolla had an overcoat rolled up and tied on the front of his saddle. The arrow struck it and cut

about fifty holes in it, and the arrowhead entered Tafolla's body just inside of the hip bone. The Indian started back, but kept turning his head and watching to see if Tafolla, whom he evidently thought he had killed, would fall. The other Indian must have been wounded; he went back first, but did not hop as lively as when he came.

[Chris Emmett wrote about Cuba Blanks in <u>Texas Camel Tales</u>:]

> No history of the Confederate-camel regime is complete without the experiences of the old Tallahassee Negro, who had walked from Indianola to Camp Verde, locating with his owners at the Ganahl Ranch, and who helped Jimmie Walker "tend the herd." Cuba Blanks, bowed with age, but clear of mind, told with enthusiasm of the days of his youth: "After the beginning of the Civil War," he began, "they were short of hands at the post, at Camp Verde, and they `pressed' me in the `CS' (Confederate Government service). I was paid nothing, though I was the same as free; got all I wanted to eat; went anywhere I wanted to go when off duty. About the same time I went over to the camp to do service, Jimmie Walker came there, too. Jim Walker left before I did. He went away from the camp as a Confederate soldier. Then I went foraging with the camels; hauled corn on them; loaded sacks on each side of them. I often went with the camels as a pack train loader during the war. Two men controlled six camels. I rode a horse on these trips, but I often rode a camel. When the camels were young, we would `break' the colts; they pitched; were hard to ride; we would hold to their hair and their humps. Jimmie Walker rode them, too. We would ride the tame ones out to the prairie

and bring them back in the evening. Candelario was there, too; he was a good man. Andre was there; he was an Arabian, and came with the camels. Also Enrico was a camel driver, but he was a half-breed Mexican. When I first went there, a man named Cloud was camel boss; then Mr. Ramsey was put in charge of the camels. Cloud was really an Indian-guide. Henry was my boss-man, and he lived at the entrance of the camel-quarters.

"There was a bunch of United States soldiers caught by the Confederates. It looked to me like it might have been six hundred of them. They were put in Prison Canyon. We had too many prisoners and we `changed' United States soldiers for Confederates.

"We herded camels in pairs; two men at a time. We had a week on and a week off."

James Washington Walker was 15 in 1862 when he came to Bandera County and herded cattle for Berry C. Buckelew for seven dollars per month. In the spring of 1863 he went to Camp Verde where he had two brothers in Lawhon's Company. He tried to enlist, but Captain Lawhon would not accept him because of his age. He spent some time herding camels before he was finally allowed to join the company in 1864. A few days later the company was commandeered by the Confederacy to guard the Texas coast.

Four companies of the former Mounted Regiment, including Lawhon's Company, were sent to the coast. In March 1865 Lieutenant Neel and 150 Confederate deserters, about half the men sent, returned to the frontier and occupied Camp Verde.
Henry Ramsey wrote to General Granger, commander of the Union occupation troops in Texas, July 19, 1865, "I have at Camp Verde 66 camels property of the United

States in my possession. I have been in charge of them since 1858, during the war and up to this time." He asked to be directed how to apply for compensation for his services.

Marvin Hunter wrote of the return of U.S. troops to Camp Verde after the war:

> While these federals were there Eugene Oborski and a man named Teinen took a contract to furnish hay for the government stock. This hay was cut in the vicinity of the place now [1922] owned by L.N. Stevens, and Mr. Walker was one of the hands employed to cut it.

The remaining camels were sold to private owners in 1866, but there were a few wild camels roaming the region throughout the 1870s. There is a story that one of these camels once ran down Bandera City's Main Street. It was subdued by a man identified only as someone who had worked at Camp Verde, perhaps Amasa Clark, Henry Ramsey, James Tafolla, or Jim Walker.

Sources: See "U.S. Army Camps In The Bandera Region."

17

Ballantyne's Rangers 1860

In March 1860, Colonel Robert E. Lee took Camp Verde's cavalry company to the Rio Grande to end the border disturbance known as the Cortina War. At this time Indian raids were numerous in the Bandera region. A couple of months earlier, Bandera County had sent a petition with 35 signatures to President James Buchanan asking for more protection from Comanches. Governor Sam Houston authorized Bandera and 22 other frontier counties to form minuteman Texas Ranger companies.

The company's hand-written muster roll included the following preamble:

> *Muster Roll of the Bandera County Minute Detachment of Texas Rangers, called into the service of the State of Texas by Hon O.B. Miles Chief Justice of Bandera County from the 29th day of March 1860, (date of this Muster) for the term of twelve months unless sooner discharged; And mustered out of the service of said state the 3rd day of July 1860, by said Hon O.B. Miles Chief Justice of Bandera County. By order of [Gen.?] Sam Houston, Governer of the State of Texas.*

Robert Ballantyne, Lieutenant
George Francis Towle, 1st Sergeant
August Pingenot, 2nd Sergeant
George Hay, 1st Corporal
Joseph T. Curtis, 2nd Corporal

Privates (10) Richard Bird, Thomas Lark Buckner, Heber Chipman, Leonard Estes, Francis Johnson, James Thomas McMurray, Thomas Lafayette

Miller, James W. Sier, William Charles Wheeler, Loammi Lemhi Wight.

Two men, Thomas Buckner and Heber Chipman, were not enrolled in the company until mid-April. In the Pioneer History George Hay listed G.W. Lewis among the rangers, so perhaps some personnel changes occurred during the company's first month.

The men rotated times of duty. Ordinarily no more than a handful of them were expected to be on scout. Governor Houston's directive to the county companies stated, "When an Indian trail is found, it must be diligently followed, and if the sign indicates a larger party of Indians than [the lieutenant] is able to cope with, he will call, not exceeding ten men to his aid." The 1860 U.S. Census captured a "snapshot" of the men who were out at that moment. The "lieut Bandera Co Rangers" had 10 men with him. (The census taker could not quite grasp the spelling of "Ballantyne")

> Robert Bassandyle, 34, Scotland, Thomas Buckner, 20, Mississippi; Charles Wheeler, 36, New York; Joe Curtis, 23, Missouri; James Sier, 32, Maryland; L.L. Wight, 21, Missouri; Heber Chipman, 18, Illinois; Frank Johnson, 23, Michigan; Francis Towle, 24, Maryland; L. Estes, 40, Mississippi.

Governor Houston stipulated that each county's ranger station should be "at some central point in the county, and not nearer than five miles of any town." Ballantyne's Company operated from Camp Winan, presumably somewhere along Winan's Creek west of Bandera City.

The state furnished five pistols to the company. The law required Lieutenant Ballantyne to post a $500 bond with the chief justice before receiving the pistols and their accessories. Each man in the company furished his own horse and had a rifle or shot gun, and a pistol. The exception was James T. McMurray who had no pistol at that time, but carried a shotgun. Richard Bird, Thomas Buckner, Frank Johnson, James Sier, and Loammi Wight carried the state pistols. O.B. Miles accounted for them upon the company's discharge.

> I OB Miles Chief Juste of Bandera County do Certify that I hav this 3d day of July 1860 Discharged from the Service of the State Lieutenant Robert Ballentyn Company Minute Detachment of Rangers in and for the County of Bandera
>
> Articles turned over was five PitaStals five Scabbard five pair moles [bullet molds] five Scrudrives hevy all the Company property turned over
>
> Witnefs my hand and Seal of the County Courte of Bandera County this 3d day of July AD 1860
>
> OB Miles
> Chiefe Justice B.C.

Governor Houston issued a statement "To the "Citizens of the Frontier" March 8, 1860, saying, "Those who have been mustered into the service will have to take script for their pay, as will also some of those who furnished supplies." Lieutenant Ballantyne apparently carried some of the company's expense. An accounting of state records in 1866 shows the state still owed him $97.32 for ranger services.

Infantry returned to Camp Verde in late May 1860. At least Bandera Pass could be closed off. The cavalry did not return until October.

Cattle rancher Robert Ballantyne was newly wed to Marinda Minear in January 1860. In 1872 he reprised his service to the county at a time of frequent Indian raids and increased outlaw activity. He led a new generation of state authorized county rangers.

Another 1860 wedding included Robert's cousin, George Hay, who married Marinda's sister Amanda. A letter from Corporal Hay in the State Archives explains how the company's muster roll came to be preserved there and, perhaps, elsewhere. The letter, with the first page missing, was written sometime after 1918.

> When our Detachment (Minute Men) Texas Rangers were Mustered into Service, as afore Said, 15 men Lieut Robert Ballantyne Cm'dg, First Sear'gt George F. Towle made three (3) Muster Rolls of Said detachment. one was filed with the Adjutant General Austin Texas, One filed in the Office of the Clerk of the County Court of Bandera County Texas. The 3rd Roll was kept by Sear'gt Towle. When the Civil War Commenced Seargt Towle joined the Army, placed the Muster Roll in my charge which I kept until the 18th day of June 1908 When I transmitted said Roll to E.M. Phelps Asst. Adjutant General Austin Texas, Who after Coppying Said Muster Roll, transmitted it to the Adjutant General of the U.S. Washington D.C. and Said Muster Roll Should now be on file in the war Department Washington D.C.

Sources

Hay, George. Letter to Unknown Addressee. Circa 1920s. Archives Division. Texas State Library. Austin.

Hunter, J. Marvin. <u>The Pioneer History of Bandera County</u>. Hunter's Printing House. Bandera. 1922.

Muster Roll. Ballantyne's Company. 1860. Archives Division. Texas State Library. Austin.

Thompson, Jerry, ed. Fifty Miles and a Fight: Major Samuel Peter Heintzelman's Journal of Texas & the Cortina War. Texas State Historical Association. Austin. 1998.

Wilkins, Frederick. Defending The Borders: The Texas Rangers 1848-1861. State House Press. Austin. 2001.

Winfrey, Dorman H. and James M. Day, eds. The Indian Papers of Texas and the Southwest: 1825-1916. Pimberton Press. Austin. 1966.

U.S. Census. Bandera County. 1860. Texas State Library. Austin.

18

The Secession Vote On The West Texas Frontier

The statewide vote on February 28, 1861, was 46,129 for secession and 14,697 against. The count was a bit closer in counties where frontier defense was an issue. Furthermore, many of the people along the West Texas frontier were from German or Polish provinces in the German Confederation. They tended to prefer a united country with a strong central government founded on a firm constitution.

The voting results from the area that became known as the Texas Hill Country were disconcerting to loyal Confederates. The following table shows the results around Bandera County

County	1860 Populations		1861 Secession Vote	
	Free	Slave	For	Against
Bandera	387	12	33	32
Bexar	10,057	1,395	827	709
Blanco *	1,183	98	86	170
Comal	3,837	193	239	86
Gillespie	2,703	33	16	398
Kerr *	585	49	76	57
Medina	1,732	106	140	207
Uvalde	497	27	16	76

The Secession Vote On The West Texas Frontier

*In 1862 parts of Kerr and Blanco counties became Kendall County.

19

Paul's Company
and
The Taking of Camp Verde

In the November 1860 Presidential election John C. Breckenridge's slavery expansion platform carried a majority in all Texas counties except Bandera, Gillespie, and Starr. The election of Abraham Lincoln led to Southern state after state seceding from the Union while the Buchanan administration marked time to the inauguration. Northern inactivity led many Southerners to believe the North would not fight.

Many expected the secession crisis to be settled peacefully or, failing that, to be resolved in a month or two by a short war. Unionists in the South made few organized efforts to counter the secession movement. In Texas, Governor Sam Houston and a few other individuals spoke out against secession.

Since the late 1850s Knights of the Golden Circle had been meeting across the South in chapters they called castles. Their avowed purpose was to extend slavery throughout the "golden circle" of the Caribbean and to uphold the Southern way of life against the Northern abolitionists. The goal of conquering all the lands surrounding the Gulf of Mexico was abandoned when KGC militias provided the Confederacy with the core of an army in 1861.

While Bandera County does not seem to have had a KGC franchise, the Medina County Knights included James Paul, a lawyer and politician who had been Henri Castro's personal secretary. By one account he had been an officer in the Texas Navy during the days of the Republic. Robert H. Williams, Medina County rancher and English immigrant, was also a member. He later wrote <u>With The Border Ruffians</u>. Gideon Thompson, one of the earliest settlers along the Anglin Prong of the Sabinal River in southwestern Bandera County, may not have been a charter member of the Medina County castle, but did serve on its committee of safety in March 1861.

The Texas Secession Convention met in Austin January 28, 1861. The convention voted for secession upon the provision that a general vote would take place in the state. In the meantime, preparations were begun to provide for the military strength to support the state's separation from the Union. A Committee of Public Safety was formed and three commissioners were sent to San Antonio to negotiate the surrender of Federal troops and property within the state.

Samuel Maverick, Thomas Devine, and Philip Luckett met with the Department of Texas commander, Brigadier General David E. Twiggs, in San Antonio. The commissioners felt some urgency to successfully complete the negotiations. Nearly a third of the Federal army was then in Texas; more than 2,000 troops were spread out among the frontier forts. Furthermore, the commissioners did not expect to get better terms from Major Carlos A. Waite, a strong Unionist from New York who was scheduled to replace Twiggs as Department commander.

General Twiggs and Major Waite represented opposite strategies among Federal forces as secession and civil war approached. General Twiggs, in the absence of explicit instructions from Washington, maintained a non-confrontational approach. Although he did all he could to uphold the honor of the army he commanded, he was from Georgia and would go with his home state when it seceded.

When the Camp Verde commander, Major S.P. Heintzelman, was transferred to Washington D.C., Major Waite was promoted to colonel and assigned to command Camp Verde. He wrote to General Twiggs and other military officials in San Antonio requesting upgrading of the camp's defenses, "Not having infantry, I respectfully request that one or two pieces of artillery--say 6 pounders, or two mountain howitzers, with a supply of spherical-case shot, canister, and round shot, together with the necessary implements (port-fire, slow-match, etc.)--may be sent here as early as practicable." General Twiggs sent a company of infantry February 4.

On the 16th, twelve days before the statewide vote on secession, Ben McCulloch and Texas volunteers seized Federal property in San Antonio. A number of KGC militia companies were among the volunteers, including a Medina County company led by James Paul. General Twiggs surrendered the U.S. Department of Texas February 18. Colonel Waite had just received notice of his promotion to head of the department and arrived in San Antonio the following day. The order had gone out to all Federal units in Texas to proceed to San Antonio in preparation of leaving the state via the port of Indianola.

Colonel Waite wished to remand the order, but it was too late. He could not effectively oppose the secessionists while the majority of his troops were marching in from the various frontier posts piecemeal. Nevertheless, he still had some hope of maintaining a Federal military presence in Texas by controlling the region between Indianola, the state's main port, and San Antonio.

Meanwhile, March 2, the three commissioners in San Antonio who had negotiated General Twiggs' surrender got word of "depredations being committed on public property at Camp Verde by some of the soldiers of company A, 1st Infantry, U.S.A." They had burned saddler and carpenter's tools and destroyed the carpenter's shop. A subsequent celebration reportedly depleted the hospital's supply of medicinal liquor.

The Commissioners in San Antonio protested to Colonel Waite that these activities were in violation of General Twiggs' agreement and dispatched a company of infantry to march towards the post. They also ordered Lieutenant James Paul of Castroville, "to repair immediately to Camp Verde with 25 mounted men."

The Medina County KGC militia had apparently been absorbed into Ben McCulloch's force and Lieutenant Paul needed to raise a new company. It was March 4 before he assembled a group of mostly Medina County men at Frank's Crossing of Hondo Creek. Their 25 names were taken down on the muster roll:

James Paul, First Lieutenant, 37
H.M. Madison, First Sergeant, 23
James B. McLamore, Second Sergeant, 19
Thomas L. Buckner, First Corporal, 21
Emanuel Widick, Second Corporal, 26

Privates

Brieten, John, 17, Niggle, Ferdinand, 42, Brook, Bernard, 25, Pingenot, August, 28, Burrows, William, 35, Ridley, V.B., 25, Downs, E.M., 41, Rine, C.C., 21, Gerdes, Henry, 19, Saathoff, Fockke, 21, Harper, M.M., 20, Vanpelt, Alison, 26, Lubbecke, A., 36, Vanpelt, George B., 28, Moore, C.R., 20, Vanpelt, William B., 25, Mott, R.C., 21, Wheeler, W.C., 45, Mylius, William, 30, Williams, R., 27

Five men from Bandera County included Thomas L. Buckner, son of Judge E.F. Buckner; August

Pingenot, a brother-in-law to Charles de Montel; and William C. Wheeler, William A. Burrows, and Doctor E.M. Downs.

R.H. Williams was among the Medina County men who signed up. William Mylius had signed the 1856 petition to form Bandera County. Bernhard Brucks, in later years, gave a brief account of the company to A.J. Sowell. After the Civil War he served many years as county judge of Medina County.

They spent the night along the Medina River in the remains of the village the Mormon Colony had abandoned in 1858. While it's not clear if the infantry ever showed up, R.H. Williams remembered 40 men in the company, including frontiersman Ed Westfall. The 15 additional men seem to have been temporary volunteers. Many of these were probably from Castroville, gathered up as the company rode through on the way to Mountain Valley (the Mormon Camp). Westfall was made provisional first sergeant and Williams became orderly sergeant.

The next morning the company set out for Camp Verde, winding northward along the Medina River, then to Bandera Pass. They made camp for the night with each side's picket guards nearby one another. The following morning Lieutenant Paul, with R.H. Williams carrying a white flag, rode up to the Federal post.

The preparations Colonel Waite had made at the camp appeared formidable as Williams observed, "strong picket defenses had been thrown up." He was sure they were in for a fight. However, the Federal troops had already received orders to surrender the post. Lieutenant Hill was in charge at Camp Verde. He made sure his men and he would leave under honorable circumstances, then surrendered and marched his company to San Antonio.

Paul's Company and The Taking of Camp Verde

Paul's Company took over Camp Verde. After some initial difficulties dealing with the camels, the men served the region as a ranger company for the rest of their enlistment. Bernhard Brucks told of the time they were chasing Indians when a cedar branch whisked off Lieutenant Paul's glasses and the whole company could not find them again. R.H. Williams remembered a Comanche raid that hit four ranches along the Guadalupe River. Coming up on the first ranch the company found two women survivors. No survivors were found at the other ranches and the company continued on the trail of the raiders four more days. Finally, the Indians were found in camp in a dense cedar brake. An early morning attack on the camp resulted in several Indians killed, the rest scattered, and 15 horses recovered.

Federal troops were shipping out from Indianola, but some were still marching in from the frontier posts and tensions remained high between Unionists and Secessionists. The possibility seemed real that the first fighting of the Civil War could break out in Texas. Governor Houston received at least two confidential Federal envoys offering between 50,000 and 100,000 Federal troops to keep him in office and Texas in the Union. While he weighed his options, Noah Smithwick, John Sansom, and other Texas Union men offered to raise companies. Finally, March 29, the governor wrote to Colonel Waite:

> I have received intelligence that you have, or will soon receive, orders to concentrate United States troops under your command at Indianola, in this State, to sustain me in the exercise of my official functions. Allow me most respectfully to decline any such assistance of the United States Government, and most earnestly protest against concentration of troops or fortifications in Texas, and

request that you remove all such troops out of this State at the earliest day practicable, or at any rate, by all means take no action toward hostile movements till further ordered by the Government at Washington City, or particularly of Texas.

President Lincoln had been inaugurated March 4, the same day James Paul was organizing his company. The new President was determined that no more Federal property in the South would be surrendered without a fight. April 14, far from Texas and Camp Verde, the opening shots of the Civil War were fired as the *Star of the West* attempted to supply Fort Sumter. Colonel Waite and his staff in San Antonio became prisoners of war. Colonel Earl Van Dorn gathered some troops and April 25 obtained the surrender of Federal troops awaiting departure from Indianola. The *Star of the West* was in port to transport the Federal troops and was captured.

Six companies of the U.S. 8th Infantry were still marching in from the frontier posts. Paul's Company was sent to monitor their progress and assess their strength. Adams' Company at Fort Inge may have been used also. Lieutenant Colonel I.V.D. Reeve, commanding the Federal force, recalled:

> From Camp Hudson to Fort Clark persons were occasionally seen on the road who appeared to be watching our movements, but said they belonged to rangers who had been on an *[Indian]* scout.

The 8th Infantry reached Uvalde May 5. By May 8 the last Federal force in Texas had reached Adam's Hill near San Lucas Springs in eastern Medina County where Van Dorn's force approached them demanding surrender. Lieutenant Paul and company were there as the Confederate State of Texas finalized military control of its territory.

R.H. Williams arranged an early discharge from Paul's Company. Although he reminisced about activities with the company through May, he was replaced on the official muster roll April 20 by a Bandera County resident, twenty-one-year-old Thomas L. Miller, who enrolled at Camp Verde. The whole company was disbanded at the end of enlistment May 16. James Paul returned to Castroville and led local militia against Indian raiders for some time. Later he was commissioned a captain and served on the War Board in Austin. R.H. Williams went on to join Duff's Partizan Rangers while Doctor E.M. Downs entered Confederate service as a surgeon. Williams and Downs would meet again in the wilderness of the Nueces region.

20

E. M. Downs, M.D.

Edwin M. Downs was of Scottish descent, born in Vermont in 1815. His wife, Caroline, was born ten years later in New York. They moved west: The Downs had reached Indiana when their first child, Edwin L., was born in 1844. The twins, H. Anne and Henriette, were born in Iowa in 1848. George W. was born in 1857, possibly in Bandera County.

That year Doctor Downs established a cattle-ranching operation between East and West Verde creeks, building a large two-story stone house five miles or so south of Bandera City. The house nestled near a spring remarkable for its surrounding grove of cottonwood trees. Another noted nearby feature was the Peach Tree Water Hole where early travelers found a peach tree growing. The ranch spread across the East, Middle, and West Verde creeks that converge and drain into Hondo Creek farther south in Medina County.

Medical care in the early days of Bandera County was mostly on the do-it-yourself plan. Anyone needing urgent trauma care usually went to O.B. Miles who had been an army hospital attendant. The arrival of Silesian settlers in 1855 brought the boon of Polish midwives. In 1857 Doctor Downs became the first M.D. in residence in Bandera County. According to one account, he saw all the patients he could get to.

Reaching patients during these frontier times could be dangerous as Indian raids came with every full moon and, not infrequently, in between. The raiders usually came in small groups and were mostly after horses, but would attack anyone caught at a disadvantage. The same year that Doctor Downs arrived, a Virginian, Bladen Mitchell, came to Bandera County to set up a horse ranch along the Medina River at 10-Mile Crossing, afterwards known as Mitchell's Crossing. He was said to have lost 400 head to Indian raids by 1869.

Since 1856 a company of the 2nd U.S. Cavalry had afforded the Bandera region some protection. The post was Camp Verde, on another Verde Creek, a tributary of the Guadalupe River, north of Bandera Pass. In 1859 Major Samuel P. Heintzelman was assigned to command the post. He traveled with his family in wagons, leaving Fort Duncan on the Rio Grande and camping out along the way to Camp Verde. He had heard of the cottonwoods in Bandera County, perhaps as a good place to camp or just for their novelty. His June 19, 1859 journal entry states, "The sixth day we encamped two miles before we got to Bandera. We intended to stop at the cotton woods, but missed them." The family was still getting settled into their new residence at Camp Verde when the major noted July 13, 1859:

> Last evening there was a man brought me a note from Dr. Downs of Cottonwood Springs 8 miles beyond Bandera, that the Indians stole some mules & mares. Lt.Graham & 12 men left this morning in pursuit.

Near the end of 1859, much of the U.S. Army in Texas, including Major Heintzelman and most of the Camp Verde troops, was withdrawn from the frontier to the lower Rio Grande area to fight the Cortina War. The reduction of Federal troops along the Texas frontier and the Republican congressional reluctance to grant additional funds for frontier defense of a slave state raised doubts along the Texas frontier about the Federal commitment to the protection of settlers.

The 1860 U.S. Census listed Doctor Downs with $10,000 in real estate and $3,830 in personal estate. He was 45, Caroline was 35, Edwin was reaching early manhood at 16, the twins were 12, and George was three. The Downs were enumerated in Castroville on the Medina County census. Perhaps the family was staying there during a time of heavy Indian raids?

Bandera County's minuteman ranger company may not have provided much reassurance. The army had returned to Camp Verde around May 1860, but the secession crisis was approaching and at the end of the year, Major Heintzelman was called away to Washington D.C. The new commander, Major Carlos Waite, began preparations for defense of the post.

In the next year the country split in civil war. In Bandera County, Doctor Downs, Charles Montague, and Judge E.F. Buckner became leading proponents of the secession movement. Charles Montague reported threats against their lives and other harassment by pro-Union men in the county.

The doctor enlisted in Paul's Company March 4, 1861 and took part in the Confederate occupation of Camp Verde. For a brief time, the company provided some ranger protection to the region. Later Lieutenant Paul and his men scouted for Colonel Earl Van Dorn as Civil War hostilities broke out and the last Union troops in Texas were taken prisoner at San Lucas Springs in Medina County. The company disbanded May 16. Interestingly Doctor Downs' age on the muster roll is 41, while his age the previous year is 45 on the census.

Age adjustments were common in the excitement of 1861. Edwin L. Downs was 17 that year, but when he joined Adams' Company, he put his age down as 18. His residence is stated as Medina County. A Bandera County lad, 16-year-old Charles Montague Jr., put his age down as 18. This company included several other

Bandera County men and served in the frontier forts west of San Antonio as far as out as Fort Lancaster.

Doctor Downs joined the Confederate States Army as a surgeon. Along with his colleagues, A.A. Ship and John Hoffman, he administered to the medical needs of the Confederacy's westernmost defense troops, including Adams' Company. They also provided medical care to some of the Texas Ranger companies (Texas State Troops) that were operating northwest of San Antonio.

The State Archives contain a number of reports these doctors made for medical discharges or furloughs. Doctor Downs was often at Camp Verde. He was at Fort Stockton on occasions. He was at Fort Lancaster to pull one of Bandera County's early settlers, Thomas Laxson, through a serious illness. Among Confederate archives, a document written in San Antonio shows he was one of three surgeons who signed a 60-day medical furlough for another early Bandera County settler, Levi Lamoni Wight.

August 10, 1862, Doctor Downs was at Fort Clark when two riders came in with an urgent call for medical assistance. A force of 94 Confederate and State Troops reaching the West Nueces River the previous evening had caught up with around 65 Union League men who were trying to get to Mexico. In the early morning hours, they engaged in battle.

The Confederate force was victorious, losing only two men dead, but had a number of seriously wounded men; some, the doctor reckoned, when he arrived on the scene that evening, "would not live to see the fort." Although nine wounded Union men had remained on the field unable to escape, Lieutenant McRae, in charge of the Confederate force, reported no prisoners taken. The names of the Union men killed at the Nueces River and of others killed later at the Rio Grande can be found on the Treue Der Union Monument in Comfort.

The next morning Confederate soldiers who expressed disapproval of the execution of wounded prisoners were among those detailed to carry the litters of the Confederate wounded. They expected to be relieved five miles or so along the way, but after a while realized there would be no relief detail. R.H. Williams provides the only eyewitness account of what happened next:

> The doctor, who was with us and behaved like a man, taking his turn at the litters, backed by some of us, at last got the men going again.
>
> [Louis] Oje and the three others of us picked up our litter and started, and the rest soon followed, the doctor bringing up the rear, to see that none lingered behind. To add to our troubles, and they were bad enough, we were in a dangerous Indian country, and had no arms with us, not even a six-shooter!

Williams remembered the groans of the wounded men. There was a little water for them, but none for the stretcher-bearers. Sometime after sundown, having trudged 15-20 miles, they finally reached terrain near Fort Clark where wagons could be sent out for them. R.H. Williams continued:

> My shoulders were cut to the bone by the litter-poles, my feet were bleeding from the sharp rocks, and I was utterly broken down, as indeed were all of us, including the doctor, though he, good fellow that he was, still had pluck and strength enough to attend to his charges directly we reached the fort.

After the war, Doctor Downs suffered from a dystrophied or paralyzed arm, perhaps due to his experience along the Nueces. Frank Buckelew remembered an incident that depicts the doctor's physical condition.

Lipan Apaches had captured young Frank near the Sabinal River in western Bandera County. He had been a captive for almost a year when he escaped and returned to Bandera County February 17, 1867:

> Just before I came home, Charles Scheidemontel, was riding a wild horse and in crossing the Medina river it became frightened and threw him off, breaking his leg. Bladen Mitchell found him and took him to his house, and went after Dr. Downs. The doctor was too feeble to go alone, so his son, Ed Downs, drove his hack for him. The three started to the Mitchell ranch, the doctor and his son in the hack and Mitchell riding a mule. They were attacked by Indians in ambush, and Ed Downs and Bladen Mitchell were both wounded, but managed to stay in the hack and on the mule. The horses became frightened and outran the Indians, and they made their way to the Mitchell ranch. The doctor had three patients instead of one. Mitchell was shot with a poisoned arrow and his recovery was slow. All three of them finally got well, but Ed Downs and Bladen Mitchell were unable to work when I got home.

Protection of settlers from Indian raids was not a priority of the Federal Army that returned to Texas to enforce Reconstruction. A company of cavalry was stationed at Camp Verde 1866-68, perhaps as a token toward the many people in the Hill Country who had remained true to the Union. But this protection was minimal and the settlers, forbidden to organize to bear arms, were hard-pressed by raiding Indians. With nothing but hard economic and political times on the horizon and fearing for life, limb, and property, many left the frontier between 1865 and 1870 when Texas Ranger companies were once again allowed.

In the spring 1867 Doctor Downs sold his land and left Bandera County with a group of other families and individuals, including David Monroe, William and Joe Curtis, and Misters Snow and Bowers. They were heading for Missouri and gathered up another family of former Bandera County residents who were then living in Burnet County. Levi Lamoni Wight remembered:

> I had a friend in Bandera, Dr. Downs, that was fiting up for going to Mo. *[He]* had considerable properety and money. Said he would take me through in consideration of my help on the way. We struck a traid. I was to drive a team of 4 yoak of oxen and take my famely on the wagon. I took a portion of the team and got my famely and joined the Dr on the Selow *[Cibolo Creek?]* 9 miles from San Antonio in May, and we were soon on the road for Mo. That Indians were marauding the country, killing and robing the frontier, was one very great cause of our desiding to make this move, and they continued for ten years after we left. A great number of men, women and children were murderd in the amediat country that we left, Burnett County and the serounding countys. These with the unsetled condision of the late trobles, was our excuse for going to another country.

Those who remained on the frontier, including Doctor Downs' son, Edwin, and the few newcomers moving in, were well positioned to take advantage of new cattle markets. Bladen Mitchell became well known throughout the region as a successful cattle rancher and trail boss.

Sources

Baker, T. Linsay. The First Polish Americans: Silesian Settlements In Texas. Texas A&M University Press. College Station. 1979.

Bechem, Robert, Brigadier General, 31st Brigade District, TST. Reports to Colonel J.Y. Dashiell. March 26, 1862; April 10, 1862; May 21, 1862; June 28, 1862; July 5, 1862; and August 7, 1863. Brigade Correspondence. Records of the Adjutant General. Archives Division. Texas State Library. Austin.

Bennett, Bob. Kerr County, Texas: 1856-1956. The Naylor Company. San Antonio. 1956.

Bitton, Davis, ed. The Reminiscences and Civil War Letters of Levi Lamoni Wight: Life in a Mormon Splinter Colony On The Texas Frontier. University of Utah Press. Salt Lake City. 1970.

Brown, John Henry. History of Texas from 1685 to 1892. Jenkins Publishing Co., The Pemberton Press. Austin & New York. 1970 [1892].

Brown, John Henry, Major, ... Frontier Organization, TST. Letter to Governor

Buenger, Walter Louis, Jr. Stilling The Voice of Reason: Texans and The Union, 1854-1861. University Microfilms International. Ann Arbor. 1979.

Dennis, Mr. and Mrs. T.S., eds. Life of F.M. Buckelew, The Indian Captive, As Related By Himself. Hunter's Printing House. Bandera. 1925.

Emmett, Chris. Texas Camel Tales. Naylor Printing Company. San Antonio. 1932.

Fehrenbach, T.R. Lone Star: A History of Texas and the Texans. The McMillan Company. New York. 1968.

Freeman, Douglas Southall. Lee's Lieutenants: A Study In Command. Charles Scribner's Sons. New York. 1944.

Glenn, Frankie Davis. Cap'n John: Story of a Texas Ranger. Nortex Press. Austin. 1991.

Hunter, J. Marvin. The Pioneer History of Bandera County. Hunter's Printing House. Bandera. 1922.

McAdoo, John D., Brigadier General, Frontier Organization, TST. Report to John Burk. December 15, 1864. Brigade Correspondence. Records of the Adjutant General. Archives Division. Texas State Library. Austin.

Menke, Jim. Military History of Medina County. Copy in DRT Library. San Antonio. 1974.

Montague, Charles. Letter to William T. Clark. July 18, 1861. Records of the Governor's Office. Archives Division. Texas State Library. Austin.

Mitchell, Bladen, Captain. Resignation Statement. April 10, 1865. Records of the Governor's Office. Archives Division. Texas State Library. Austin.

Mott, Samuel C, Private. Resignation Statement. April 10, 1865. Records of the Governor's Office. Archives Division. Texas State Library.

Muster Roll. Adam's Company.

Muster Roll. Lawhon's Company. Mounted Regiment. Texas State Troops. April 30, 1863. Archives Division. Texas State Library. Austin.

Muster Roll. Mitchell's Company. Frontier Organization. Texas State Troops. June 1, 1864. Archives Division. Texas State Library. Austin.

Muster Roll. Paul's Company. 1861. Archives Division. Texas State Library. Austin.

Neel, Lieutenant. Letter to Major John Henry Brown. March 25, 1865. Records of the Governor's Office. Archives Division. Texas State Library. Austin.

Quarterly Return of Commissioned Officers, 31st Brigade District. June 1, 1862 and October 10, 1862. Brigade Correspondence. Records of the Adjutant General. Archives Division. Texas State Library. Austin.

Rodriguez, Jose Policarpo. <u>Jose Policarpo Rodriguez: "The Old Guide"</u>. Publishing House of the Methodist Episcopal Church, South. Nashville & Dallas. 1898?

Scott, Robert N., et al, eds. <u>The War of the Rebellion, A Compilation of Official Records of the U.S. and Confederate Armies</u>. 70 volumes in 128 books. Government Printing Office. Washington. 1891.

Smith, David P. <u>Frontier Defense in the Civil War: Texas' Rangers and Rebels</u>. Texas A&M University Press. College Station. 1992.

Smith, Thomas T. <u>The Old Army In Texas: A Research Guide to the U.S. Army in Nineteenth-Century Texas</u>. Texas State Historical Association. Austin. 2000.

Smithwick, Noah. The Evolution of a State or Recollections of Old Texas Days. N.N.P. Gammel. Austin. 1900.

Sowell, A.J. Early Settlers and Indian Fighters of Southwest Texas: Facts Gathered From Survivors of Frontier Days. Ben C. Jones & Co. Austin. 1900.

Thompson, Jerry, ed. Fifty Miles and a Fight: Major Samuel Peter Heintzelman's Journal of Texas & the Cortina War. Texas State Historical Association. 1998.

Tyler, Ron, et al, eds. The New Handbook of Texas. Texas State Historical Association. Austin. 1996. Six Volumes.

Underwood, Rodman L. Death on the Nueces: German Texans: Treue der Union. Eakin Press. Austin. 2000.

Williams, R.H. With The Border Ruffians: Memories of the Far West: 1852-1868. J. Murray. London. 1907.

Winkler, William, ed. Journal of The Secession Convention of Texas1861. Austin Printing Company. Austin. 1912.

Wooster, Ralph A., ed. Lone Star Blue and Gray: Essays on Texas in the Civil War. Texas State Historical Association. Austin. 1995.

Wooster, Ralph A. Texas And Texans In The Civil War. Eakin Press. Austin. 1995.

Tobin, Peggy, ed. "Frontier Reminiscences." The Bandera County Historian. Vol. 6. No. 3. (Summer 1983) Pages 1-2.

Young, Kevin R. <u>To The Tyrants Never Yield: A Texas Civil War Sampler</u>. Wordware Publishing, Inc. Plano. 1992.

21

Charles Montague Letter

Bandera County 19th July/61
To His Excellency
Gov. Clark
Austin

I am Sorry to trouble your Hon. about the affairs of our County, but I hope to be excused when I State that the most of our Settlers paid no taxes this year, that a document was handed round to get Signatures for a remodelling of this government, So as to form a Union of the States again, that no officer of the county took the oath of allegience, but the Clerk of the District Court [W.S. Goodwin?], and that a Polander who intertained the Hon Judge Buckner for two nights was cursed next day for interating a Secefsionist, and that the judge's buggy wheel was Stolen & his cushin and thrown in the river, that a resolution was pafsed at a meeting of theirs at the mormon field to hang Judge Buckner, Doctor Downs, and myself.

About a fortnight Since, I Sent a man round with a paper for Signatures for the call of a meeting to organize a militia company and take the Oath of aligience of this State and the C.S. There was pretty good attendance, but they posativily refused to take the oath and would not enrol themselves as militia, but formed a home guard, which in case of invasion may prove of a dangerous character.

Will your Hon. give me or any one Else authority to enrol [these?] as a militia company, or give me Such directions as your Hon. may deem advisable under the circumstances.

Your obt. Servant. Chs. Montague
Justice of the Peace
Bandera County

P.S. Our Souther[n] boys have almost all joined Capt. Adams Company and the Secfsionists are in a minority in the County at this time.

P.S. 2nd. The postmaster in Bandera (a german) has not taken the Oath, and is a great Union man. Hon. Judge Buckner dropt a letter in the office for me and next day I got it, and it was torn open in the Office before I got it. Can this be remedied?

When the county organized in 1856, August Klappenbach, a Bandera merchant, was elected Clerk of the District Court and later held other county offices. About the same time, he married Mina Kuhue of Castroville and formed a partnership with Charles de Montel to run the commissary at Camp Verde. He was appointed by Governor Sam Houston to be the county's first notary public and Bandera's first postmaster.

Sixteen-year-old Charles Montague Jr. left Springhill College, a Jesuit school in Alabama, to enlist in Adams Company. After the war his 10-12 years service as county clerk left a creditable mark on the history of Bandera County.

In 1857 Doctor Edwin Downs and family established a ranch along East Verde Creek south of Bandera City at Cottonwood Springs. Doctor Downs built a two-story stone house there. It was said that he treated all the patients he could get to. He served in Paul's Company and later was a surgeon in the C.S.A. His son, Edwin L. Downs, served in Adams' Company.

Eliphalet Frazer Buckner, born in Kentucky in 1810, had established a law practice in San Antonio and Castroville in the 1850s. He was elected district judge of the 18th Judicial District in 1856. The district included Bandera, Medina, Atascosa, Uvalde, Kenny, and Maverick counties. In 1860 he bought land and built a house in Bandera County, but left the area in 1862 to move back to Kentucky.

His son, Thomas Lark Buckner, served in Paul's Company, Adams Company, and later went to Austin where by account he was elected lieutenant in a company raised for the C.S.A. He returned to Bandera County after the war and taught school on Bandera Creek.

Judge Buckner's daughter, Betty, can be found in the Journal of the Secession Convention along with several other young Austin ladies presenting a hand-sewn Texas flag to the convention.

While some Bandera County men joined Adams' Company, others with Union sympathy reluctantly formed the required militia unit, but continued a passive resistance to the Confederacy. The election of Bladen Mitchell as captain of the home guards, with his Virginia accent and fervent Southern loyalty, probably deflected suspicions of disloyalty whenever the question arose.

22

Bandera Resolutions 1861

The Daily Ledger and Texan.
Friday, July 26, 1861. San Antonio

At a meeting of the citizens of Bandera County held at the Court House in said County, July 10th, 1861, for the purpose of organizing a Military Company for home protections, Hon. E.M. Ross was called to the chair and W. G. Goodwin, chosen Secretary.

On motion it was resolved, that a Committee of three be appointed to draft Resolution expressive of the sense of this meeting with regard to certain reports derogatory to the character of the citizens of this county as good and loyal citizens of the South. Messr. W. G. Goodwin, P.D. Saner and O. B. Miles were designated as said Committee and reported the following preamble and resolutions.

Whereas, Reports have been circulated detrimental to the character of the inhabitants of this county as good and loyal citizens of the South, thereby bringing Bandera county into discredit: and, Whereas, while many of the neighboring frontier counties voted *against*, Bandera county cast its vote *for* Secession, and whereas, although being on the frontier and requiring the services of every man at home to defend the families and property of its citizens from a merciless, savage foe, yet Bandera county has already furnished for the Regular company, eighteen brave, active and intelligent men, of fully one third the entire voting representation.

Therefore:

Resolved: That we denounce all such reports as malicious slanders.

Resolved: That having no sympathy with Abolitionism in any of its forms we pledge the services of every citizen of the county in defense of our country and homes against invasion from all foes, *red* or *whites*.

Resolved: That we challenge the State to show a county which has done or will do more in proportion to its ability in defending our Common Country against the aggressions of all enemies, native or foreign.

Resolved, That copies of the above preamble and resolutions be forwarded by the chairman of this meeting to the Galveston News, San Antonio Herald, and Ledger and Texan, with request to publish.

On motion the above were unanimously adopted. A company of Home Guards was then organized consisting of 30 members. Capt. O. B. Miles, 1st Lieutenant, Robert Ballantyne, 2nd Lieut., Thos. Bandy. – Muster and drill every Saturday.

EDWARD M. ROSS, Chairman.
Attest, W.G. Goodwin, Secretary

23

The Bandera Home Guardes
And The Third Regiment of
The 31st Brigade District

Bandera County's 1860 U.S. Census population of 399 was probably a little undercounted. Indian raids were frequent that year and the census taker hurried through. He found many residences empty. The names of some of the county's citizens may be found on census rolls of safer places like Castroville and San Antonio. The Downs family, for instance, can be found on the Castroville census.

The following year, shortly after the 33 to 32 county vote for secession, Doctor Edwin Downs and a handful of other Bandera County men left to serve in the Confederate Army. From that point on, Union men held a slight majority.

In the summer of 1861, some county residents were refusing to pay Confederate taxes. They held meetings and passed around petitions for rejoining the Union. When Charles Montague complained to the governor, the Union men, mostly army veterans, placed a notice in Texas newspapers assuring neighbors that they were not abolitionists.

Charles de Montel, a Medina County rancher, surveyor, and one of the founders of Bandera City, was a fervent Secessionist. His influence in Medina and Bandera counties is believed to have subdued some Union feelings. Nevertheless, the Confederate State of Texas fretted about Hill Country Unionists, particularly those in Gillespie County and parts of Kerr, Blanco and Kendall counties.

In 1861 Texas was divided into 33 brigade districts as a way to oversee the home guard units of the various counties. During the next year, the brigade structure began to take shape as individual companies formed and soon would be organized into regiments. Hopefully, for the South, they would be ready to support the regular Confederate troops in case of a Yankee invasion of Texas. Later, the brigade districts were utilized to help administer the draft.

Bandera County was in the 31st Brigade then being organized by Brigadier General Robert Bechem, Texas State Troops, headquartered in New Braunfels. All or parts of 22 counties comprised the district including Blanco, Kendall, Comal, Medina, and Kerr.

General Bechem was a reluctant citizen-soldier appointed to a difficult and thankless bureaucratic position. He had been a consignment merchant before the war. He found his new job quite frustrating. He said the time it took up ruined his business, yet he did not seek personal gain from his office because, "I disliked too much the way money was made by Speculators, Agents, etc." While writing often to ask for a hardship discharge, he took every opportunity to postpone the required election of brigadier general which would confirm his position. Nevertheless, it seems, he made his best effort to perform his duties.

The brigade generals reported directly to the Adjutant and Inspector General in Austin, Colonel Jeremiah Yellot Dashiell. The former newspaper editor provided the generals with advice, directives, and interpretation of the C.S.A. regulations.

The mail between New Braunfels and Austin usually took no more than two days, but dispatches between New Braunfels and the various frontier locations in the district could take weeks. General Bechem complained to Colonel Dashiell, March 26, 1862, "Enrollments from the Counties of Bandera, Edwards, Mavarick, Dawson, Kimble and of several precincts in the Counties of Llano, San Saba & Atascosa are still wanting and from other Counties the returns of election for Company officers have not been made, which detains me in completing the organization of this Brigade."

While some frontier counties could not raise enough men to form a company, other more populous counties could fill their own regiments. Gillespie County raised six companies that comprised the 2nd Regiment. Medina County raised enough companies to form its own brigade under the command of H.J. Richarz. Bandera County mustered enough men for one company and one squad (perhaps 65-120 men). The county was grouped with several other counties that were to form the 3rd Regiment.

The Bandera Home Guardes organized in March with the election of officers taking place March 30, 1862. It was April 10 before General Bechem could report that a company had formed in Bandera County and April 15 before he could report the results of the election of officers for that company. (The spelling of guards with an "e" may be noted. Anything French conjured up images of Napoleonic military élan for both North and South.)

For captain, the men elected Bladen Mitchell, who began his horse ranch in 1857. J.P. (Polly) Rodriguez remembered him as a firm supporter of the Confederacy. While it might be expected that the majority would have elected a Union man, the choice may reflect some kind of compromise between Bandera County's Union and Confederate sympathizers. In addition, his Virginia accent might have soothed the suspicions of a snooping provost marshal.

A cattle rancher, Scottish-born Robert Ballantyne, came with Lyman Wight in 1854 and served as 1st lieutenant. His cousin, George Hay, was 2nd lieutenant while R.S. Perkins served as junior 2nd lieutenant.

Many of the county's Polish and Mormon men served in the company. Polly Rodriguez, offered the rank of captain in the C.S.A., chose instead to serve as a private in the home guards, "It was our business to defend the neighborhood from the wild Indians and to keep down the disorderly element at home. I served four years, the whole period of the war, in this company. We were almost constantly on the scout, and had many unimportant encounters with the Indians." In George Hay's reminiscence, the men chased after many raiding Indians and sometimes caught up with them. It did not help, however, that the gunpowder available to them was of inferior quality.

Due to the large German-speaking population of the district, the military law was distributed in English and German copies, but there was a shortage of both. There does not seem to be any record that Captain Mitchell ever received one. Although supposed to be organized and operated according to C.S.A. regulations, the frontier companies were very democratic affairs. George Hay, a storekeeper in Bandera City at the time, later recalled, "Being an officer made no difference to me. I went into the ranks, stood guard and performed all the duties of a private."

Another event of April 1862 did not bode well for the sparsely settled frontier regions. The Conscription Law went into effect and the home guard units became the main source of draftees for the Confederate Army. By June General Bechem was reporting that there were few men eligible for conscription remaining in some of the counties of his district and "no enrollments made in the Counties of Zavalla & Concho & only a small number enrolled in the Counties of Bandera, Kerr, Mason, Frio & Uvalde."

The men of Mitchell's Company resorted to a practice that was not uncommon along the frontier. As late as February 1864 they were still padding the company roll with ineligible members like 64-year-old Paul Martin and 66-year-old Daniel Arnold. General Bechem related the same to Colonel Dashiell August 7, 1863, "I am sorry to say that in some Companies the commanding officers in making up their Rolls for the draft have not been very particular but have added the names of persons who were over age or otherwise by law exempted. Some of them were drafted & had to be withdrawn from the list; but at the other hand, about an equal number of such illegal names will be among the remaining undrafted."

General Bechem's organizational process came to a brief halt in the summer of 1862. Election of field officers for the regiments was supposed to take place June 7. The returns for the 3rd Regiment were late and puzzling. The six companies, between five and six hundred men, abstained. Only a portion of Kendall County voted, sending a message that if General Bechem understood, he did not say. Expressing only his usual bewilderment and frustration, July 5, he pronounced the Brigade organization completed: "Not having succeeded to organize the 3d Regiment composed of: 1 Company Blanco County (southern portion), 3 Kendall, 1 Kerr (eastern portion), & 1 Bandera [,] as with the exception of 1 Poll (Sisterdale) no election for Field officers has been held, and not being authorized by law, to make appointments for these offices, I better defer ordering a new election until the Conscripts may have been ordered into service, and considering the regimental & battalion organization completed, I intend in the course of this week to order in compliance with Sect. 13 of the military law an election for Brigadier General to take place on Saturday August 9th a.c." He won the election unopposed and the brigade structure seemed ready to settle into routine matters.

Unfortunately for all General Bechem's organizational efforts the events of the Civil War outpaced the usefulness of the militia structure he had struggled to complete. The Confederacy's requirement for men was enormous and desperate. After the August 1863 elections the Tenth Legislature of Texas took up the question of turning over the Mounted Regiment of Texas Rangers to the C.S.A. This would leave the militia units of the frontier counties alone to face Indians, deserters, and outlaw gangs. Those companies along the frontier would have to be reorganized to face the challenge.

General Bechem protested to Colonel Dashiell August 18, "Besides the five Counties of Comal, Blanco, Kendall, Medina & Gillespie, where the additional 25 per cent (resp. 50% of the undrafted men) have to be drafted, I would then have to order the enrollment & draft for organization for the local defences in the following 8 Counties of my District viz: Kerr, Mason, Llano, San Saba, Bandera, Atascosa, Uvalde & Maverick, which would again take up my time for several months with writing orders, corresponding, investigating petitions and exemptions, granting furloughs etc., etc."

General Bechem was spared the agony of reorganizing the frontier counties. September 17, Bandera County sent a set of resolutions to the governor that foreshadowed the state's solution for frontier defense: They suggested a county ranger company and exemption from the draft.

Sources

Baker, T. Lindsay. The First Polish Americans: Silesian Settlements In Texas. Texas A&M University Press. College Station. 1979.

Bandera Resolutions of 1863. Brigade Correspondence. Records of the Adjutant General. Archives Division. Texas State Library. Austin.

Bechem, Robert. Letters to J.Y. Dashiell: 3-26-1862, 4-10-1862, 4-15-1862, 5-21-1862, 6-11-1862, 6-28-1862, 7-1-1862, 7-5-1862, 8-7-1863, 8-18-1863. Brigade Correspondence. Records of the Adjutant General. Archives Division. Texas State Library. Austin.

Hunter, John Marvin. The Pioneer History of Bandera County. Hunter's Printing House. Bandera. 1922.

Montague, Charles. Letter to William Clark. July 19, 1861. Records of the Governor's Office. Archives Division. Texas State Library. Austin.

Muster Roll. Mitchell's Company. Texas State Troops. February 6, 1864. Archives Division. Texas State Library. Austin.

Quarterly Return of Commissioned Officers, 31st Brigade District. 6-1-1862 and 10-10-1862. Brigade Correspondence. Records of the Adjutant General. Archives Division. Texas State Library. Austin.

Rodriguez, Jose Policarpo. Jose Policarpo Rodriguez: "The Old Guide". Publishing House of the Methodist Episcopal Church, South. Nashville & Dallas. 1898?

Smith, David P. Frontier Defense in the Civil War: Texas' Rangers and Rebels. Texas A&M University Press. College Station. 1992.

Stephens, A. Ray and William M. Holmes. Historical Atlas of Texas. University of Oklahoma Press. Norman. 1989.

Tyler, Ron, et al, eds. <u>The New Handbook of Texas</u>. Texas State Historical Society. Austin. 1996.

U.S. Census. Bandera County. 1860. Geneology Division. Texas State Library. Austin.

U.S. Census. Comal County. 1860. Geneology Division. Texas State Library. Austin.

U.S. Census. Medina County. 1860. Geneology Division. Texas State Library. Austin.

24

Diphtheria On The Civil War Texas Frontier

Diphtheria (*Corynebacterium diphtheriae*) was a major cause of death among children under 10 years of age during the 19th century. In the worst cases, lesions form in the throat which swell, often to the point of slowly strangling the victim. The procedures of tracheotomy and intubation were familiar to some medical practioners of the day, but neither was widely used before the 1880s. Moreover, the toxic effects of the disease often lead to kidney and/or heart failure, making all efforts futile. A variety of remedies were in use before antitoxins were discovered in the mid 1890s: Calomel (mercurous chloride) was sometimes used as a treatment; lemon juice was frequently an ingredient in other remedies. Outbreaks of diphtheria were common worldwide until mass immunizations were administered after World War II.

Communicable diseases of all sorts were rampant across the United States as the Civil War broke out and men from all regions came together to form armies. While survival of the diseases was considered part of basic training, men who lived, but remained too ill to serve, were often sent home on medical furlough or discharge. At the same time, as men became increasingly scarce along the Texas frontier, many women and children from outlying regions moved in with friends and relatives in larger communities.

Of two frontier counties known to have had diphtheria epidemics during the war, Gillespie County had an 1860 population of 2,736, while Bandera County had

399. When the Texas counties organized home guard units in 1862, Gillespie County formed six companies while Bandera County raised enough men for one company and one squad. The home guards were the source of draftees for the Confederate Army and the Bandera Home Guards shrank from around 100 men in March 1862 to 53 by February 1864.

Diphtheria broke out in Gillespie County sometime in the last few months of 1861. An unidentified correspondent wrote to the <u>Neu Braunfelser Zeitung</u> for January 4, 1862 edition:

Fredericksburg, Texas Dec. 9, 1861

> Health conditions so far as grown people are concerned are very good however among children here death has demanded considerable toll. There is here a sickness among children that often results in death. The children get sore throats and noses the latter often being totally stopped up; their breath becomes laden with bad odor; breathing becomes cumbersome; ulcers form in the throat of the children which becomes putrid. The sickness often does not last long, especially when medical attention is given immediately; but often it lasts a long time and then the illness is usually fatal. We have here a very good physician, Dr. Keidel; sad to say however the people live so scattered that his help often comes too late. Though he saved many, many died. Almost every day some children were buried. I also had a sick child but he is on the road to recovery.

Two men are recorded as having treated the diphtheria patients in Gillespie County. Doctor Wilhelm Victor Keidel was born and educated in Germany where he received his medical degree. After coming to Texas he served six months in the U.S. Army during the U.S.-Mexican War. When he moved to Fredericksburg in 1847, he was Gillespie County's first M.D. and served a term as Chief Justice. He was 47 years old in 1862 when he was appointed surgeon for Gillespie County's regiment of home guards. Like Doctor Keidel, Christian Althaus had settled his family in Fredericksburg in 1847. Although not an M.D., he was skilled in concocting remedies and had received medical training while in the Prussian Army. He was 41 years old in 1862 and a second lieutenant in Company C of the Gillespie County home guards.

By the end of 1861, diphtheria had killed 147 Gillespie County children. Thirteen more had died when the Fredericksburg correspondent wrote to the New Braunfels paper for its January 24th edition:

> My neighbor has lost all of his children. Dr. Keidel saves many. Day and night he is busy bringing help wherever possible.

In 1856 Levi Lamoni Wight and Sophia Leyland had been the first couple to marry in Bandera County. Lamoni was serving in the Confederate Army along the Texas coast, while Sophia stayed at the Bandera Hotel with their two toddlers and newborn. She wrote to her husband November 9, 1862:

> every body in town is sick. Benjmin has gone for that man that cures the sore throat. His children are all sick and two more of Charley they don't expect to live.

Among the large Bird family that moved to the Bandera region with the Lymon Wight Colony in 1854, Benjamin Bird had recently finished a term as a county commissioner and no longer exempt, was probably in the home guards at this time. Charles and Bernice Bird lost three children in the epidemic: James, age five, died October 23rd; Helen, age 12, October 31st; and David, age 10, November 11th. Sophia Wight wrote to her husband November 16th:

> We are all well at present but every morning I dread to look in the children mouths for fear of finding ulcers in them. There is 2 or 3 new cases every day but they seem to understand it so well now that is not so dangerous. Mr. Althouse has been here and shoed Miles how to do but the cure is almost as bad as the decese.

According to family tradition in Gillespie County, the government had sent Christian Althaus to Bandera and the medicine he administered contained honey, almond juice, and the bark of the blackjack oak. He may have stayed in Bandera City a few days or weeks. Thirty-four of 35 patients were alive when he left. Sophia Wight wrote in her November 16th letter:

> They only lost one case and that was Charly's oldest boy. He died and was bueryed the day before he got home. Marrion's baby has got it verry bad and bud McKay has had it and they are boath here and the children are likely to have it any day. I have kept them as close as posable but I am so afraid of it I can hardly rest and to think of the baby's having it is worse than all because the cure would kill her she is so small but we will have to trust to Providence to be merciful (blurred ink) is not a case. Andrew's oldest girl has got it but is getting better. It would take a sheet of paper to tell all that has got it.

Orlando B. Miles and his family had lived in Bandera City since 1853. He had received medical training as a hospital attendant in San Antonio during his last days of service in the U.S. Army. Anyone in the Bandera region who had been wounded by an arrow usually went to O.B. Miles for treatment. The value of his medical experience and dedication was heightened by the fact that Doctor Edwin Downs, the county's only M.D., was serving as a Confederate surgeon along the line of frontier forts from San Antonio to El Paso. Miles was 37 years old and in his third term as Chief Justice when Sophia Wight wrote,

> It takes Miles all the time to tend the sick. He goes from morning till night and hardly takes time to eat.

Blackjack bark notwithstanding, more deaths verified as or possibly attributable to diphtheria are recorded: Daniel Rugh, a blacksmith, livestock raiser, and county sheriff, had moved his family to Bandera City in 1860. During 1862, the youngest two of four Rugh daughters died in the epidemic. December 1, 1862, Benjamin and Mary Bird lost George, age seven. Willie, age six, son of O.B. and Diana Miles, died June 25, 1863. Amasa Clark, in Bandera since 1853, had married Eliza Jane Wright of Fredericksburg in 1859. He was a county constable when they lost their first two children, Annie and Amasa Jr. By this time Sophia Wight had moved to Burnet County with relatives. She wrote to her husband December 18, 1864:

> The last we heard from Bandera they still had a great deal of sickness there. Mary Bird lay at the point of death and they had hoping cough and dypththera. Mr. Clark lost two children in 2 weaks. I am afraid we will get it here. It is at Taits

and Wartons. They have all had it. Mrs bob Tait lost a little babe with it.

Sources

Alberti, P.W., MB, Phd, FRCS (C). "Tracheotomy Versus Intubation: A 19th Century Controversy." Ann Otol Rinol Laryngol. 93:1984:333-337.

Bechem, Robert, Brigadier General, TST. Report to Adjutant General J.Y. Dashiell. April 10, 1862. Brigade Correspondence. Adjutant General Records. Archives Division. Texas State Library. Austin.

Bitton, Davis, ed. The Reminiscences and Civil War Letters of Levi Lamoni Wight: Life in a Mormon Splinter Colony On The Texas Frontier. University of Utah Press. Salt Lake City. 1970.

Clark, Amasa Gleason. Reminiscences of a Centenarian. Naylor Company. San Antonio. 1930.

"Correspondence." January 4 and January 24, 1862. The Neu Braunfelser Zeitung. New Braunfels.

Denson, Mrs. Howard, Mrs. Billy Burnes, and Mrs. Howard Graves. Bandera Cemetery Records. Bandera County Historical Survey Commission. Bandera 197?.

Election Returns. Bandera County. 1861-1864. Archives Division. Texas State Library. Austin.

Hardy, Ane. "Tracheotomy Versus Intubation: Surgical Intervention In Diphtheria In Europe and the United States, 1825-1930." Bulletin of Historical Medicine. 66:1992:536-559.

Hunter, J. Marvin. The Pioneer History of Bandera County. Hunter's Printing House. Bandera. 1922.

Muster Roll. Mitchell's Company. Frontier Organization. Texas State Troops. February 6, 1864. Archives Division. Texas State Library. Austin.

Quarterly Return. 31st Brigade District. July 1, 1862. Brigade Correspondence. Adjutant General Records. Archives Division. Texas State Library. Austin.

Slade, Daniel Denison, M.D. Diphtheria: Its Nature and Treatment, With An Account of the History of Its Prevalence In Various Countries. Blanchard and Lea. Philadelphia. 1861.

Turk, T.R. Mormons In Texas: The Lyman Wight Colony. Port Lavaca? 1987. Copy in DRT Library, San Antonio.

Tyler, Ron, et al, eds. The New Handbook of Texas. Texas State Historical Association. Austin. 1996.

25

The Incident at San Julian Creek

When the siege of Vicksburg ended July 4, 1863, a flood of deserters, mostly Confederate and some Union, spread across the Texas frontier. While some headed for California and others for Mexico, the growing numbers of deserters and draft dodgers who sought refuge in the remoteness of the Texas frontier proved worrisome to the state government. Texas State Troops (Texas Rangers and home guard units) were directed to arrest deserters, whenever found, and turn them over to Confederate authorities. A few commanders instead ordered summary executions out of exasperation, overzealous patriotism, or just meanness of spirit.

The latter case seems exemplified by the actions of William J. Alexander, commander of the Southern Division of the Mounted Regiment. This regiment of Texas Rangers formed early in 1863 from the remnant of the Frontier Regiment. Major Alexander made his headquarters at Camp Verde, the ranger station for Lawhon's Company.

The 69 men of Lawhon's Company (June 1863) were about evenly divided in their opinions about the war, but were united in their desire to protect their families and neighbors from Indian raids. They were mostly from Bandera, Blanco, Medina, and Uvalde counties. Most had been in Montel's Company before the reorganization of the regiment into smaller companies. While some left to enter the Confederate service and others joined their home guard units, many remained to serve in Company B, Lawhon's Company.

The Incident at San Julian Creek

Of the 13 Bandera County men in Montel's Company, only six remained to serve in Lawhon's Company: William Ballantyne, Richard Bird, Thomas O. Messer, Joseph Onion, and William Charles Wheeler. Lamoni Lemhi Wight, one of Lyman Wight's sons, served some time in Lawhon's Company, but later transferred to the Bandera Home Guardes.

Captain Charles de Montel left with hopes of commanding a commerce raider. The men of Company B elected their former first sergeant as captain. John Lawhon and his wife, Jean, came from South Carolina and were among the early settlers of Blanco County. Captain Lawhon had been foreman of Judge W.E. Jones' ranch before the war.

In the 1920s, J. Marvin Hunter, journalist-historian of Bandera County, pieced together the story of the Williamson County men: "This party of eight men and a boy passed through Bandera, and stopped here for a day or so, resting their horses and buying such supplies as they needed on the trip. They did not make any secret of their destination or the cause of their going, but openly stated that they were on their way to Mexico, to avoid conscription."

Hunter gathered his version of the story from several Bandera old-timers who had seen the bodies and knew most of the men in Lawhon's Company. He reworked the account many times over the years, publishing the story in the <u>San Antonio Express</u> and the <u>Houston Post,</u> as well as in his own magazine, the <u>Frontier Times</u> and in his book, <u>The Pioneer History of Bandera County</u>.

Additional details can be gathered from the perspective of Williamson County. Clara Scarbrough's history of that county includes an account of the men who traveled to Bandera City during the Civil War. At least two of the men were not avoiding conscription for they were already serving in Confederate cavalry regiments. William M.

Sawyer, whose farm was near Georgetown, enlisted in Company D, Gurley's Regiment July 8, 1862. His brother, Coston J. Sawyer, enlisted March 26, 1862, in Company A, Morgan's Squadron. The other men in the group included George Thayre, brother-in-law of William Sawyer, and William Shumake, Jack Whitmire, Jake Kyle, John Smart, and a Mr. Van Winkle. The unnamed boy's age is variously given as 13 to 16 years old.

Indeed, some of the men in the group may have been leaving Texas to avoid the draft and the boy was approaching draft age. The Sawyers may have been deserting, but a descendent of William Sawyer, family historian Daniel Mahler, provides another possibility. According to family tradition, the Sawyer brothers were on furlough and, with their companions, were going to Mexico to buy horses to bring back to their companies. The price of horses in Texas had risen with the inflation of Confederate currency; however, horses could be purchased at a reasonable price in Mexico. Eight to nine hundred dollars had been raised among the men for that purpose.

When they bought supplies in Bandera City, their wealth apparently became public knowledge. Major Alexander, in his headquarters at Camp Verde, heard that these men had passed through the town. He began pursuit with 25 men from Lawhon's Company.

Several days later the Williamson County men were finishing their noon meal in camp on Squirrel Creek in Medina County when Major Alexander overtook them. According to the Hunter account, "Maj. Alexander stepped out into an opening, and swinging his saber over his head, called upon them to surrender, telling them that he had them surrounded and there was no chance for them to escape, and if they would quietly submit he would pledge his word that they should have a fair trial by court-martial at Camp Verde."

The Incident at San Julian Creek

Actually, State Troops such as Alexander's were obligated by orders to turn over any deserters or draft dodgers to Confederate authorities. The major had no jurisdiction to court-martial Confederate troops or civilians, but what he eventually did was much worse.

The rangers and their prisoners set out for Camp Verde. Two days later, July 25, 1863, they had reached San Julian Creek a couple of miles southeast of Bandera. Camp was made for the night. Scarbrough's account says that alcohol was provided for the men that evening. The major remained quiet while one or more surrogates incited a lynching. Almost half the men objected strenuously, but were overruled. Nine men left the camp rather than participate.

A horse-hair rope was used to hang the men from a tree branch, one at a time. Apparently, a horse was used to haul each victim off the ground. As each man stopped kicking, the rope was cut from his neck. A new loop was made and placed around the neck of the next man. When only William Sawyer remained alive, the rope had become quite short and he requested that he be shot instead of hanged. In Hunter's several versions, most say that one man shot Sawyer, but one says a firing squad shot him. Whichever is right, alcohol intoxication is strongly suggested, for Sawyer was only hit in the arm by the rifle shot or volley fired from a short distance. He fell face down. Someone hastily reloaded, forgetting to remove the ramrod, and fired into Sawyer's back, killing him.

The next day was Sunday and about 8 o'clock, Bandera residents noted Alexander and his hung-over men riding through town with some extra horses and mumbling something about having gotten rid of some bushwhackers. ("Bushwhacker" was the Texas Confederate term for anyone who hid out in the cedar brakes to avoid the draft.) A short time later Joseph Poor had been looking for a lost horse along San Julian Creek when he saw the bodies lying about and the ramrod looked like an arrow. He raced into town to report Indians in the country.

A group of townsmen gathered to go out for an investigation. Among them were several officers of the home guard, including, Robert Ballentyne, George Hay, and O.B. Miles. Sheriff Daniel Rugh asked Constable Amasa Clark to come along. They found seven bodies with short pieces of rope tight around their necks and one with a ramrod protruding from his back. George Hay recalled the ramrod, "had passed entirely through his body and penetrated into the ground for at least 10 to 12 inches. It was with great difficulty that I drew out this ramrod."

John Pyka was 16 years old when he helped bury the Williamson County men, "We dug a shallow grave, laid the dead men into it, spread blankets over them and covered them up the best we could with dirt and stones to keep the wolves from getting to the bodies." He also recalled, "Their pockets were empty, showing that they had been robbed. A 16-year-old boy that was captured with the men was spared for the time being, I understand, and taken up about Fredericksburg, but as he was never heard of again, it is supposed that he, too, was killed."

Many years later, Henry Nowlin, son of Dr. James C. Nowlin, wrote a letter to J.S. Piper, husband of William Sawyer's daughter, Ellen, "Do you and Ellen know that the young boy when released by the mob on Julian came directly to Curry's Creek and spent the night with us." Apparently, the boy was an uncle of Ellen's, on her mother's side, but his name is not mentioned in the letter.

The one or more surrogates who instigated the hangings for Major Alexander remain unknown, but one prime suspect emerges from the scant details available: Daniel Malone had enrolled in Montel's Company from Medina County and served as first corporal. On the first

The Incident at San Julian Creek

muster roll for Lawhon's Company, Malone is listed among the privates. He was appointed third corporal, July 25, 1863, by Major Alexander's Special Order Number 48 as noted on the company's August muster roll. Former Third Corporal L. Brewer was reduced to the ranks.

Interestingly an "inspection of arms" listing the company weapons June 9, shows Malone carried an army pistol and a "five Shooting Rifle." The rifle would have been a rare Patterson Colt with a revolving cylinder like the pistol. For what it's worth, that could eliminate Malone as the ramrod shooter.

In 1865, Bandera County citizens commissioned Henry White, a stone mason, to place a tombstone at the gravesite. He engraved it with the men's names and a traditional rhymed verse that dates at least to 1376, "Remember, friends as you pass by; as you are now, so once was I. As I am now, you soon will be; prepare for death and follow me."

G.H. Noonan was District Judge of the region when the Reconstruction government directed grand juries to investigate war atrocities and injustices. April 24, 1866, a grand jury in Bandera County indicted "W.J. Alexander, et al" for murder and robbery. George Hay declared, "I have seen many foul crimes in my time, but this was the most revolting that I ever knew." Amasa Clark called it cold-blooded murder.

As the warrants went out, the indicted men began to leave the region. New Braunfels law officers killed Daniel Malone when he resisted arrest, but all the others disappeared. The case continued to be carried "on the docket" from term to term for many years. In 1870, Governor E.J. Davis required county sheriffs to report any outstanding arrest warrants in their counties. August 3, T.C. Rine reported for Bandera County:

In district Court Spring Term AD 1866 Indictiment for Murder and highway Robbery against WJ Alaxander supposed to be in Matamoris Mexico.

Sylvester Stayton, RD Cude, FL Cooper, Wm Gray, Augest Gralin, Adan. Bleaker Whereabouts unknown.

HD Peden supposed to be in Illinois.

John Carson, Cal Putman, FM Casner, Osker Johnson, SC Westfall, Peter Zorger, Daniel Stayton whereabouts unknown.

Danl Malone dead.

Sources

Glenn, Frankie Davis. Capt'n John: Story of a Texas Ranger. Nortex Press. Austin. 1991.

Hunter, John Marvin. "A Bandera County Tragedy." Frontier Times. (August 1924) Pages 8-11.

Hunter, John Marvin. "Bandera Mass Hanging Was Diabolical." The Houston Post. October 17, 1937.

Hunter, John Marvin. "Lonely Graves and Sentinel Oak Mark Grim Tragedy of Bandera Hills." The San Antonio Express. January 19, 1922.

Hunter, John Marvin. The Pioneer History of Bandera County. Hunter's Printing House. Bandera. 1922.

Inspection of Arms. Lawhon's Company. June 9, 1863. Mounted Regiment, Texas State Troops. Archives Division. Texas State Library. Austin.

Jordon, Terry G. Texas Graveyards: A Cultural Legacy. University of Texas Press. Austin. 1982.

Mahler, Daniel D. Phone Conversation Regarding the San Julian Creek Incident. October 9, 1995. Jolly, Texas.

Monthly Return. Lawhon's Company. Mounted Regiment. Texas State Troops. August 1863. Archives Division. Texas State Library. Austin.

Muster Rolls. Lawhon's Company. Mounted Regiment. Texas State Troops. Archives Division. Texas State Library. Austin.

Muster Rolls. Montel's Company. Frontier Regiment. Texas State Troops. Archives Division. Texas State Library. Austin.

Nowlin, Henry M. Letter to John Samuel Piper. October 22, 1941. www.rootsweb.ancestry.com~txbander/. (Accessed 11-22-16)

Receipt for cotton and woolen carders (signed by Peter Zorger). Bandera County. March 28, 1864. Records of the Governor's Office. Archives Division. Texas State Library. Austin.

Report of Crimes. Bandera County. August 3, 1870. Adjutant General Records. Archives Division. Texas State Library. Austin.

Scarbrough, Clara Stearns. <u>Land of Good Water</u>. Williamson County Sun Publishers. Georgetown. 1973.

Smith, David P. <u>Frontier Defense in the Civil War: Texas' Rangers and Rebels</u>. Texas A&M University Press. College Station. 1992.

Wilcox, A. Letter to Charles de Montel. March 22, 1863. Montel Papers. Center for American Studies. UT Austin.

26

The Bandera Resolutions 1863

At a meeting of the citizens of Bandera Co holden Sept 17th 1863, O.B. Miles, Chief Justice in the Chair the following resolutions were adopted.

Resolved--

That every able bodied man, embracing the larger part of our voting population, who could leave our County have long since gone to the war, most of them volunteering as soon as active hostilities commenced, and all that now remain are necessarily compelled to do so to provide food for helpless women and children, and to preserve their lives and property from the frequent and ruthless raids of our merciless savage foes. It is only by unceasing vigilance we are able to keep them in check--every man now taken from our County would leave a point exposed, and were any number taken a short time only would elapse before every house both in the settlement and around it would be in ashes, and the women and children massacred or carried to a captivity worse than death. Troops stationed miles away are powerless to prevent such atrocities, they know it only when the deed is done, our only defense lays in ourselves and each other.

Resolved--

That we are ready and willing to serve our State and Country to the extent of our ability in defending our homes and resisting invasion by Indians or other foes, and respectfully petition the Govenor of our State to authorize O.B. Miles, Chief Justice of our County, to organize a Volunteer Company for this purpose.

Resolved--

That the Company after organization shall mount, arm, equip and provision itself, and shall be put in such a state of efficiency that it will give a good account of itself, whatever foes our homes may be attacked by, asking pay from the State for such time only as our Company or Scouts from it shall be actually in the field.

Resolved--

That a copy of these Resolutions be forwarded to the Govenor and that his early and favorable attention be respectfully and earnestly entreated to the same.

O.B. Miles, Chairman
Leml. Hayward, Secretary

27

Three Letters and a Crisis

The declining number of men on the Texas frontier during the Civil War became an increasingly serious issue in the last months of 1863. The Frontier Regiment of Texas Rangers that had served during 1862 had been reorganized in reduced form as the Mounted Regiment for 1863. Despite the official name change, the regiment was still often referred to as the Frontier Regiment and sometimes as McCord's Regiment after its commander, Colonel J.E. McCord.

During 1863 the State of Texas, in an attempt to get the national government to pay for frontier defense, made arrangements to turn this regiment over to the Confederacy. In March 1864, it became the 46th Texas Cavalry Regiment. The implications for frontier citizens were ominous.

With Chief Justice O.B. Miles as chairman and Lemuel Hayward as secretary, Bandera County citizens held a meeting September 17, 1863, to discuss the situation. They drafted a set of resolutions to the governor asking for approval of an independent county minuteman ranger company. They resolved in careful language aimed at the Confederate draft:

> That every able bodied man, embracing the larger part of our voting population, who could leave our County have long since gone to the war, most of them volunteering as soon as active hostilities commenced, and all that now remain are necessarily compelled to do so to provide food for helpless women and children, and to preserve their lives

and property from the frequent and ruthless raids of our merciless savage foes.

As Union invasion forces threatened Texas borders, the Confederacy needed additional troops. Private Levi Lamoni Wight was with Company C, 1st Texas Cavalry, stationed along the Texas coast:

> In Feb of the following year (64) we were ordered on force march to reinforce Tom Green and Waker [Walker] who was then retreting up read river followed by Genl Banks of the fedral forse. We had ben during the winter months so fare on the gulf cost holding the fedral gun boats at bay. Now that the boats were called away to New Orleans in consideration of a heavy campaign through Louisanna and Texas.

The Federal force advanced up the Red River in Louisiana supported by gunboats. The Federals anticipated a shermanesque march through Texas. However, when General Banks moved away from the river and his gunboat support, he was turned back at Mansfield April 8, 1864. The next day another Federal retreat followed the battle at Peach Orchard (Peach Tree Hill). Casualties were high on both sides as Private Wight remembered the subsequent battle at Pleasant Hill, "brave men melting before the blazening cannon and charging Infantry one volley after another and dead men were in piles."

John Lawhon's Company stationed at Camp Verde was among the four companies of the Mounted Regiment that were called away from the frontier to guard the Texas coast when regular Confederate coastal troops were sent to the Red River. The men of Lawhon's Company had been recruited mostly from Bandera, Blanco, Kerr, Kendall, Medina, and Uvalde counties. Men from Bandera

County included William Ballentyne, Richard Bird, H. Chipman, Thomas O. Masser, Joseph Onion, Loammi Lemhi Wight, and William C. Wheeler.

A minuteman ranger force pieced together from the frontier county home guard units was planned as a replacement for the full-time rangers. The Frontier Organization, as the minuteman regiment was called, was not quite in place when the Mounted Regiment companies left the frontier.

Confederate officials received numerous calls to return the companies or at least Lawhon's company. Doctor Edwin Downs, probably on his way to or from one of the frontier forts, took time to write a letter from Rio Hondo, Medina County. Bandera sent W.A. Lockhart to San Antonio to confer with Confederate authorities. He was asked to write down his concerns so that they could be forwarded to higher officials.

Colonel McCord, the regimental commander, was at Camp Verde May 2, 1864, where he had overseen the transfer of four of his companies to coastal defense duty. He wrote to Major General J.B. Magruder of his concerns for the portion of the frontier being left open to Indian raids, "The frontier will be broken up, and the outer line be thrown back to San Antonio and Austin, from 80 to 100 miles inside of the present line." Although an organization of frontier county militia companies was forming, Colonel McCord suspected the loyalty of these home guard men, many of whom had relatives among the pro-Union men, draft dodgers, and deserters who hid out beyond the frontier. Confederates referred to these men as "bushwhackers." The colonel concluded:

> In my opinion, general, it is of the utmost importance that one company at least should be ordered to the permanent occupation of Camp Verde, for the twofold purpose of protecting the camels, some

80 in number, belonging to the Confederate States, and for the protection of the surrounding country. That district is a key to several counties, and its occupation will afford protection to a large section of country.

May 11, 1864 another officer of the regiment, Captain H.T. Edgar of Company F, was among those who made representations to Lieutenant Colonel A.G. Dickenson, the Confederate adjutant general in San Antonio. Captain Edgar stated his concern for the people in the region from Camp Verde to the Rio Grande who were "destitute of any protection whatever, save the militia." He recommended that at least one company of the regiment be left in place. Furthermore:

> This company should in my opinion be composed of men acquanted with all the water holes and whose interests are identified with that portion of the frontier.
>
> And as Captain Lawhorn's company is composed chiefly of the bona-fide citizens of this frontier, I would move that they be assigned to that duty in preference to any other company, believing, as I do, that they would give universal satisfaction.

[From Dr. E.M. Downs]
Rio Hondo, Tex., May 11, 1864

Col A.G. Dickenson:
Sir: In the capacity *[of]* commander of this frontier when stationed here, you manifested so much interest in our protection *[that]* you will excuse me asking you to use your influence with the commanding general of this department to continue the protection necessary to secure the lives and property of the loyal citizens of this frontier. Within two weeks and since the removal of the troops

from Camp Verde, the Indians have made two visits to this neighborhood, killed two good, loyal citizens, killed and driven off nearly all our horses. We are not only exposed to the depredations of the Indians, but our worse foe the renegades and organized members of the Union League. We have very little confidence in the present partially organized troops of the frontier, as we believe many of them are men that have fled from the interior to avoid conscription and are and have been from the first, and are friends and sympathizers with the deserters and renegades that infest the mountains of this frontier and the Rio Grande.

We are fully convinced that regular troops only can keep down the spirit of disloyalty and vengeance that exists among the renegades that infest this frontier. Believing that you will generously use your influence in our behalf, and knowing as you do our dangerous and exposed situation, I have appealed to you. Camp Verde is the key to protection to all this portion of the frontier. If consistent to do so we would beg that Captain Lawhorn's company, with one other good company, be placed at Camp Verde, as we have full confidence in them as true, loyal Southern men and prompt and energetic in driving out the Indians. Captain Lawhorn's company has the entire confidence of all the loyal citizens of this frontier.

Very respectfully, your obedient servant,
E.M. Downs

[From W.A. Lockhart, Bandera County resident:]
San Antonio, May 11, 1864.

Lieut. Col. A.G. Dickinson:

Sir: I address you upon a subject of vital interest to our whole western frontier, stretching from the Colorado River to the Rio Grande. The withdrawal of the Frontier Regiment, and especially of the troops stationed at Camp

Verde, has left the inhabitants wholly defenseless, being exposed not only to Indian depredations, which are now of frequent occurrence, but to the still more dangerous and destructive depredations of deserters, jayhawkers, and robbers, who already infest the whole country from the Colorado to the Rio Grande. Without some force to protect this frontier I have no doubt the whole country west of San Antonio will be deserted by every loyal citizen, and the beeves and horses in this region will be driven to Mexico, seized and carried off by the Indians, or destroyed. I live 4 miles beyond Bandera and 8 miles from Camp Verde, and I have no hesitancy in saying that if there be not at least one company of troops kept stationed at Camp Verde, or in that neighborhood, not only I but every loyal citizen in that part of the country will be sacrificed or compelled to abandon the country and fall back to San Antonio in less than sixty days. Already robberies and murders are of frequent occurrence.

On Monday night last Capt. William Wallace, an old Texan and one of our best and most skillful Indian fighters, was killed not more than 20 miles west of San Antonio, and very far within the lines of the frontier.

This was by Indians, who at the same time stole most if not all of his horses. It was only a week previous to this a party of Indians made their appearance on the Hondo, 30 miles west of San Antonio, and killed one man and scattered and drove off a large number of horses. But these occurrences have become so frequent that it would require too much space to mention all. Another danger equally as great, if not greater, threatens us on this frontier in our present defenseless condition, and it is from the vengeance threatened to every loyal citizen by the friends of the disaffected who have been forced to leave the country to avoid military service; nothing but the presence of an armed military can restrain this class of persons, and especially if their renegade friends and relations should return, as they would be sure to do if the military force be wholly withdrawn from this frontier. I address you, colonel, hoping you may use your influence at headquarters to secure us in our need some protection, and knowing that you are not unacquainted with our condition, I appeal to you in earnest language, because I am deeply impressed with a sense of the danger which now threatens every settler on the frontier. His life and property are daily at stake.

I rely on your influence because as a commander of this district you have ever appeared solicitous to protect the frontier. As the State troops or militia have been turned over to the Confederacy by the Governor, we of the frontier think we have a right to demand protection from the general commanding the department. I have no doubt Captain Lawhorn's company, formerly stationed at Camp Verde, if ordered back would give great satisfaction to the frontier inhabitants, at least to the loyal portion of them.

Very respectfully, your obedient servant,
W. A. LOCKHART.

[Endorsement:]

Respectfully forwarded, for the information of the major-general commanding, with the remark that many verbal representations being made upon this subject. He is an intelligent gentleman, and his views and representations worthy of consideration.

A. G. DICKINSON,
Major and Assistant Adjutant-General.

William A.A. "Big Foot" Wallace joined the Confederate Army March 1, 1864. He served as lieutenant in a company raised in Medina County by Charles de Montel for Rip Ford's Cavalry of the West. These troops rushed to the Rio Grande to repel a Union invasion. Wallace's sudden departure from the region may have sparked the rumor that Indians had killed him. The rumor was apparently widespread, but Big Foot Wallace died an old man in 1899. Ben Batot was an 18-year-old Medina County home guard ranger when he heard the rumor. In later years, he told this story to A.J. Sowell:

> While we were in camp at Moss Hollow, about six miles below D'Hanis, we received a report that the Indians had killed Big Foot Wallace. It was about twenty miles to where Wallace lived [on Chicon Creek], but we immediately set out, about ten of us, and arrived at his place about dark. His lonely little cabin was deserted, no one there, and all we found in the way of provisions there was a small piece of bacon and a little corn meal in a sack. We prepared to camp, and in about an hour Big Foot Wallace came strolling in with his gun over his shoulder, his two pistols in his belt, his Mexican blanket on his arm, and leading his horse.

The men of the four ranger companies that were sent to the coast felt useless in their new position. Some were being used as wagon freighters. Near the end of March 1865 about half of them deserted and occupied Camp Verde in an effort to be placed back into the frontier service where they could protect their homes and families.

28

The Frontier Organization

Anticipating the imminent withdrawal of the Texas Ranger companies from the frontier, the Confederate State of Texas made arrangements to transform the home guard units of the frontier counties into minuteman ranger companies. The Frontier Organization, as the new ranger force was called, faced increasing Indian raids as well as deserter and outlaw gangs.

The frontier people petitioned and protested against the removal of the full-time ranger companies. Nevertheless, in March 1864, four companies of the Mounted Regiment, including Lawhon's Company from Camp Verde, were sent to the Texas coast replacing regular Confederate troops that were rushed to Louisiana. A Federal force moving up the Red River threatened to invade Texas. In a series of battles, the Federal advance was halted, but at great cost. Private Levi Lamoni Wight remembered a portion of the fight at Pleasant Hill, "we charged and from one single volley one half of our men fell to a man."

Left in place of the Mounted Regiment companies was a hastily rearranged assortment of the county home guard companies along the frontier. An act of December 15, 1863, formed 59 counties from the Red River to the Rio Grande into the Frontier Organization. The act exempted these counties from the Confederate draft and directed their home guard units to organize into companies of 25-65 men with a captain and two lieutenants. Each company was to divide into roughly equal-size squads that would rotate time of service. The entire company could be called out in an emergency.

The Frontier Organization

The counties of The Frontier Organization were divided into three districts with a major of cavalry appointed to command each. In the northern or 1st Frontier District was Major William Quayle, headquarters Decatur. The central or 2nd Frontier District was commanded by Major George Bernard Erath, headquarters Gatesville. The southern or 3rd Frontier District which included Bandera County was commanded initially by Major James M. Hunter, headquarters Fredericksburg.

The companies, as first formed, averaged 50-55 men each. In Bandera County O.B. Miles drew up a muster roll February 6, 1864, showing the following names, ranks, and ages for Mitchell's Company:

Captain Bladen Mitchell, 27
1st Lieutenant Orlando B. Miles, 37
2nd Lieutenant Robert Ballantyne, 35

Sergeants
 Jackson M. Phillips, 33
 W.H. Mott, 28
 F.M. McKay, 19
 George Hay, 27

Corporals
 Thomas Bandy, 45
 Loami Lemhi Wight, 30
 Joseph Sutherland, 23
 Albert Adamitz, 19

Privates (42)

Walek Aunderwald, 28; Daniel Arnold, 66; Benjamin F. Bird, 36; Charles Bird, 38; Samuel Bird, 28; Ezra Alpheus Chipman, 46; E.P. Chipman, 19; S.F. Christian, 37; A.J. Click, 55; Meachem Curtis, 46; John Dugozs, 46; Horace V. Freiman, 21; Nicanor Garcia, 40; Erineo Gonzales, 38; Santos Gonzales, 42; W. S. Goodwin, 36; John Green, 23; Alexander Hay, 18; Lemuel Haywood, 37; Andrew Hoffman, 37; Albert Hiduke, 49; Thomas Hiduke, 31; F. Juritzke, 37; Casper Kalka, 49; Joseph Kalka, 28; August Klappenback, 46; Blas Loya, 33; Henderson C. McKay, 46; Paul Martin, 64; Thomas Mazourick, 46; K. Merit [Merrets], 36; J.B. Miller, 46; Joseph Moravitz, 32; Joseph H. Poor, 37; Antone Pyka, 43; S.J. Rine, 56; Thaddeus C. Rine, 30; Jose Policarpio Rodriguez, 34; Edward Merritt Ross, 48; Daniel Rugh, 30; Patterson Douthit Saner, 41; Francis Woclawcyzk, 39

Each of the 53 men armed and equipped himself. All were armed with muzzle-loading black powder rifles or shotguns. Twenty-five men had rifles and pistols, while seven had shotguns and pistols. Twelve had only rifles and nine had only shotguns, probably the double-barrel type. The total armaments for the company were 37 rifles, 16 shotguns, and 32 pistols. The state provided some powder and percussion caps, but as George Hay pointed out, the quality of the powder was often poor.

The men rotated turns at patrolling or "scouting", usually serving about ten days out of each month. Bladen Mitchell's ranch house may have served as their ranger station. Taylor Thompson, captain of a company in an adjacent county, related a story of his Civil War ranger experiences. While looking for a lost horse, he said, "I found twelve or fifteen men there preparing to start on a scout the next morning." The ranch was located along the east side of the Medina River ten miles from Bandera City. Mitchell's Crossing of the river is now under the north part of Medina Lake.

The Confederacy did not recognize the state's right to grant exemptions from the draft. Governor Pendleton Murrah sparred with President Davis over the issue until the end of the war. Three men of Mitchell's Company have the letter "d" by their names on the February muster roll, perhaps indicating that they had been drafted: Nicanor Garcia, Erineo Gonzales, and A.J. Click. However, of the three, only A.J. Click's name does not appear on the company's next muster roll.

Confederate authorities criticized the Frontier Organization as an unnecessary diversion of troops from the C.S.A. and as a haven for deserters and draft dodgers. Contrary to the conscription law, the muster roll of Mitchell's Company, and those of many other companies, included names of men ineligible for the draft. When those names were chosen for the draft, the county got a brief reprieve from loss of manpower.

New muster rolls were drawn up in an attempt to allay some of the allegations against the Frontier Organization. Paul Martin, 64, was spry enough to freight corn to Camp Verde, but his name does not appear on the muster of June 1, 1864. Captain Mitchell, rather than O.B. Miles, was enrolling officer and listed 13 fewer men than in February:

Captain Bladen Mitchell, 28
1st Lieutenant O.B. Miles, 37
2nd Lieutenant Robert Ballentine, 35

Sergeants
  J.M. Phillips, 34
  W.H. Mott, 28
  F.M. McKay, 19
  George Hay, 27

Corporals
  [blank]
  Benjamin Bird, 36
  Joseph Sutherland, 23
  Loami L. Wight, 30

Privates (30)

Walek Anderwald, 28; Charles Bird, 38; George Calvert, 37; Ezra A. Chipman, 46; E.P. Chipman, 19; R. Click, 33; John Dugos, 46; Horace V. Freiman, 21; John Green, 23; Nicanor Garcia, 40; Santos Gonzales, 42; Erineo Gonzalez, 38; Alexander Hay, 18; Andrew Hoffman, 37; Thomas Haiduck, 31; Albert Haiduck, 49; F. Juretzke, 37; Casper Kalka, 49; August Klappenback, 46; Blas Loya, 33; Thomas Mazourick, 46; K. Merretts, 36; J.B. Miller, 46; J.

Moravitz, 32; Henderson C. McKay, 46; Jose P. Rodriguez, 33; Daniel Rugh, 30; T.C. Rine, 30; P.D. Saner, 41; F. Waclawcyzk, 39

June 20, after a continuing series of crises in the 3rd Frontier District, Governor Murrah appointed Brigadier General John D. McAdoo to take charge. The higher caliber officer could take over the administrative burden while the district's major could be more active in the field. General McAdoo had served with the 20th Texas Infantry earlier in the war and had administrative experience as an assistant adjutant general of state troops in Houston. Since March he had been in command of the 6th Brigade District.

General McAdoo arrived in Fredericksburg June 23 and called his captains to a two-day conference to discuss problems and solutions. He then made an inspection tour of the district, trying to bolster morale along the way.

Apparently, Mitchell's Company did not patrol outside the county boundaries before 1864. In April of that year Major Hunter had organized a scout of 60-75 men from the companies of his command and sent them to the upper Llano River region in an attempt to thwart raids from deserters, outlaws, and Indians. When General McAdoo took command, he assigned specific areas for each company to patrol on a regular basis. The headwaters of the Llano River seem to have been assigned to Mitchell's Company. Taylor Thompson remembered:

> I was in camp with a party of rangers some sixty miles to the northwest of Bandera. One day I left camp alone to hunt deer, and about 10'oclock that morning I met the Captain Mitchell above referred to. He was scouting in that same section with a squad of his company, for that was the territory assigned to him for scouting duty, while I was

merely passing through, returning from having followed an Indian trail through there.

Polly Rodriguez recalled the circumstances when a detachment of Mitchell's Company captured three deserters who were on foot near the headwaters of the Llano River:

> The captain had to put a guard over them to keep them from killing themselves eating. They were as ravenous as wild animals. We did not let them have all they wanted for about three days. In that time they had begun to change wonderfully. They were sound and well soon, and Captain Mitchell gave them up to the Confederate authorities. He was a great friend of the Confederacy, and did all he could to help them.

By December 1864, General McAdoo was commanding the 2nd and 3rd Frontier Districts. He was still working to improve the effectiveness and morale of the Frontier Organization in his districts. After reducing the threat of various gangs of outlaws, deserters, and renegades in the Fredericksburg area, he set about to face an expected increase in Indian raids. He wrote to the state's new Adjutant and Inspector General, Colonel John Burk, December 15:

> The Indians are in the country. One hundred are known to be between this point and the headwaters of the Medina. The whole available force of the District has been ordered out, and are now in pursuit. As yet, their depredations, as reported to me are not considerable, excepting the killing of two women, whom they happened to encoun-

ter alone and at some distance from any settlement.

Our forces may push them too closely to allow of much damage being done, but I fear they will escape, as heretofore, without receiving any signal punishment. I am preparing a General Order for the Districts under my command, for a System of Service which will remedy existing defects, and enables us hereafter to meet these forays more successfully, if not effectually stop them--I will transmit you a copy in a few days.

Corporal Loami Wight's wife was staying with other Wight family members in Burnet County. His sister-in-law, Sophia Wight, wrote to her husband December 18:

> Loami is here. He has been here about three weaks. He was in Bandara 20 days. He had the chills when he came here. He is better now but is waiting for clothes. He will leave the last of the weak. His time is out. There is about half of the Reg on Sick furlow. They are verry mytch discouraged and he thinks there will a great many disert if they are not better provided for.

Although popular among his German neighbors, the hard-pressed Major Hunter eventually resigned. January 19, 1865, John Henry Brown was appointed major for the 3rd Frontier District. Earlier in the war Major Brown had served on General Ben McCulloch's staff and later served on General Henry McCulloch's staff, but illnesses and a surgery had kept him from active duty much of that time.

Some men from Mitchell's Company took part in the last campaign of the Frontier Organization. These men were out on the fringes of the frontier long after Lee surrendered in April. The men of the Frontier Organization gave the Texas frontier the best protection they could manage under very difficult circumstances and with very few resources. George Hay looked back over the years:

> I have never received a cent for my services and none of my comrades ever received a cent of pay. We had to furnish ourselves, too. Some ammunition was supplied, but it was of such poor quality as to be almost worthless. The Indians often made raids down into this settlement and below here, and we would take their trail, sometimes inflicting severe punishment on the red rascals.

[General McAdoo issued General Orders Number 3 to the Third Frontier District in December 1864:]

For the purpose of rendering the service of the Frontier Organization uniform throughout the different counties of this command; to increase the efficiency of the service and to facilitate concentrated and combined movements of the troops when necessary, it is ordered by the Brig. Genl. Commanding:

I) That within each county or company district, there shall be established a permanent camp or rendezvous; and that the different companies be divided into four squads of as nearly equal strength as possible, which said squads shall succeed each other in the scouting service regularly every ten days; that each squad be required to report promptly at the said company camp on the day the preceding scout is to be relieved.

II) When said camps are located the company commanders will forthwith notify the commander of

	the district of its location, and also the company commander in all the adjoining counties.
III)	It shall be the duty of the officers in command of said camp, to keep the forces thus collected constantly on scouting service, in those districts in which Indians, Bushwhackers, and Deserters are likely to be found--detailing from said force a sufficient number of men only, to keep camp and act as couriers, should it be necessary to communicate with neighboring camps on the appearance of Indians or other contingency.
IV)	It shall be the duty of the officers in command of the camp detail, to dispatch immediately to the nearest county camp, by swift courier, any intelligence he may receive of Indians, or other danger threatening the Frontier, and such camp will communicate in like manner with the next, until the whole Frontier line is informed.
V)	When Indians are known to have penetrated the settlements, the different scouts will guard particularly the passes through which they usually go out with horses. All experience has shown that the most effective plan of operations against an Indian enemy is to head off the raidng parties as they leave the settlements with their plunder and booty. If they are able to get in through the scouting lines, see to it that they go out without spoils, and with severe punishment.
VI)	When camps are located they will not be changed without good reasons therefore, and when changed, the district commander and company commanders in the adjoining counties, will be notified of the location of the new camps. The commander of the district will be notified of the nearest Post Office to the different camps.

The Frontier Organization

VII) The companies of Captains Gussett and King and Lieut. Haynes and Herring will form one common camp to be selected by Captain King. The companies will cooperate in the scouting service, and senior officers present commanding the men on duty.

VIII) When Indians have penetrated the settlements, the company commanders may call out a portion of their command not on their regular tour of duty, and if necessary the entire strength of their companies for the emergency. Let the Indians find themselves met by armed forces, not only on the outer line of the Frontier, but everywhere within those lines.

IX) The greatest promptness and diligence are enjoined upon the officers and men of this command. The Brig. Genl. commanding has good reason to believe the Indians of the North-West are incited and perhaps led to depredate on the Frontier of Texas by White men, who are agents, if not officers and soldiers of the United States. Extra efforts and watchfulness should be at that period in each moon, when Indians usually visit our Frontier. The country expects her Frontier Organization to protect the Frontier, and the Brigadier General commanding calls upon every officer and every man, to see to it that the public expectation is not disappointed.

By Command of Brig. Genl. J.D. McAdoo
Russell DeArmond
Maj. & A.A.A.G.

31st Brigade District   3rd Frontier District

(All or parts of the following counties)

31st Brigade District	3rd Frontier District
Atascosa	Atascosa
Bandera	Bandera
Blanco	Bee
Comal	Blanco
Concho	Burnet
Dawson	Dawson
Edwards	Dimmit
Frio	Edwards
Gillespie	Frio
Kendall	Gillespie
Kerr	Karnes
Kimble	Kerr
Kinney	Kinney
Llano	LaSalle
Mason	Live Oak
Maverick	Llano
McCulloch	Maverick
Medina	McMullen
Menard	Medina
San Saba	Uvalde
Uvalde	Zavala
Zavala	

    Some of these counties were unorganized or had become depopulated during the Civil War. The preliminary boundaries of Edwards County had been laid out, but no county seat had been designated and no government had been organized.

29

The Last Campaign

In the early morning of April 9, 1865, the Army of Northern Virginia was making a last desperate march. Ahead along the Lynchburg Road General John Gordon led the Second Corps in an attempt to break through to a railroad line where supplies might be found. Around 8 o'clock General Gordon sent word to his commander: "Tell General Lee I have fought my corps to a frazzle, and I fear I can do nothing unless I am heavily supported by Longstreet's corps." But Longstreet's corps was fighting the rear guard action and the remnants of a proud army were assailed from all sides by overwhelming Union forces. That afternoon General Robert E. Lee dressed in his finest uniform and set out on Traveler to meet General Ulysses S. Grant at Appomattox Court House.

At the same time, over 1,000 miles away in Texas, Major John Henry Brown, of the 3rd Frontier District, was unaware of the recent events in Virginia. Confederate authorities in Texas were concerned about the large numbers of draft dodgers, deserters, and various renegade elements that populated the outer reaches of the Texas frontier. Major Brown had received orders a month before to assemble about a quarter of the district's rangers for a sweep through the outer frontier. On this day he left his Fredericksburg headquarters as planned, to gather his ranger forces at Camp Verde for what would be the last campaign of the Frontier Organization.

The morning of April 10, as Captain Bladen Mitchell and Bandera County's detachment of rangers came over Bandera Pass, they would have seen a slightly bizarre pastoral scene as two herders drove dozens of camels onto the slopes to graze. Horses unaccustomed to camels did not respond well to the sight of them. Captain Mitchell and his men managed their startled horses and continued past the camel camp. For some of the war, Texas Rangers stationed at Camp Verde made their camp two miles downstream from old Camp Verde where Doctor James Nowlin once had a ranch house. Captain Mitchell would find Major Brown there.

Less than half the expected 400 men showed up. From 22 counties only 183 men described as "Americans, English, Irish, French, Poles, Germans, and Mexicans" showed up at Camp Verde with their 243 horses and pack animals.

Also unexpectedly Major Brown had to accept the resignations of Captain Mitchell and Private Samuel Mott of the Bandera detachment. They stated their intentions of going to Houston to enlist in the Confederate Army. Major Brown advised the Governor, "Under ordinary circumstances, I should be compelled under a sense of duty to recommend the non-acceptance of this resignation. Capt. Mitchell is a good officer, but the patriotism which prompts his course merits praise and I therefore respectfully forward & recommend the acceptance of his resignation." Of Samuel Mott's resignation the major said, "Approved and respectfully forwarded with the remark that Mr. Mott has been recommended to me as a true & good man, as I know his brother, Marcus F. Mott, to be."

The next day with two 10-man squads ahead to protect the flanks, Brown's battalion rode to Kerrville, turning west to follow Johnson's Fork of the Guadalupe River, then north. The objective was to scout the area between the upper San Saba and Concho rivers and engage a large force of deserters reported to be gathering there to raid the settlements.

April 21 the battalion arrived at deserted Fort McKavett on the San Saba River. After a two-day rest the men moved out to scout the area. They encountered several small bands of deserters and rustlers and took prisoners when they could be caught.

At the end of April, the battalion was scouting in detachments along the upper Guadalupe and Llano rivers. Lieutenant Lacey's detachment found a group of men described as "bushwackers" holed up in a brushy creek bottom. A fierce firefight erupted which lasted most of the day as others of Major Brown's detachments arrived to reinforce Lieutenant Lacey. When it was over Brown's men had seven prisoners, two bushwackers were dead and at least two had escaped. The battalion reached the end of the campaign at Fredericksburg early in May after three and a half weeks on horseback.

At Fredericksburg the men learned of Lee's surrender and Major Brown disbanded his battalion: the Bandera men and others went home. Their discharge date is May 3. Major Brown and a small detachment continued on to Austin with about 30 prisoners. When they arrived in Austin, they found a chaotic situation as Governor Pendleton Murrah and other officials had left for Mexico. Major Brown disbanded the remainder of his men and released the prisoners, "under a pledge that they would peaceably return to their respective homes."

Sources

Bennett, Bob. Kerr County, Texas: 1856-1956. The Naylor Company. San Antonio. 1956.

Bitton, Davis, ed. Reminiscences and Civil War Letters of Levi Lamoni Wight.

University of Utah Press. Salt Lake City. 1970.

Brown, John Henry. History of Texas from 1685 to 1892. Jenkins Publishing Co., The Pemberton Press. Austin & New York. 1970 [Originally 1892].

Boyd, Eva Jolene. Noble Brutes: Camels On The American Frontier. Republic of Texas Press. Plano. 1994.

Emmett, Chris. Texas Camel Tales. Naylor Printing Company. San Antonio. 1932.

Freeman, Douglas Southall. Lee's Lieutenants: A Study In Command. Charles Scribner's Sons. New York. 1944.

Hunter, John Marvin. The Pioneer History of Bandera County. Hunter's printing House. Bandera. 1922.

McAdoo, John D. Letter to John Burk. December 15, 1864. Brigade Correspondence. Records of the Adjutant General. Archives Division. Texas State Library. Austin.

Mitchell, Bladen, Captain. Resignation Statement. April 10, 1865. Records of the Governor's Office. Archives Division. Texas State Library. Austin.

Mott, Samuel C, Private. Resignation Statement. April 10, 1865. Records of the Governor's Office. Archives Division. Texas State Library.

Muster Roll. Mitchell's Company. Frontier Organization. Texas State Troops. June 1, 1864. Archives Division. Texas State Library. Austin.

Muster Roll. Mitchell's Company. Frontier Organization. Texas State Troops. February 6, 1864. Archives Division. Texas State Library. Austin.

Rodriguez, Jose Policarpo. <u>Jose Policarpo Rodriguez: "The Old Guide"</u>. Publishing House of the Methodist Episcopal Church, South. Nashville & Dallas. 1898?

Smith, David P. <u>Frontier Defense in the Civil War: Texas' Rangers and Rebels</u>. Texas A&M University Press. College Station. 1992.

Tobin, Peggy, ed. "Frontier Reminiscences." <u>The Bandera County Historian</u>. Vol. 6, No. 3. (Summer 1983) Pages 1-2.

30

Frank Buckelew

In early spring 1866 the red buds were in bloom when Frank and Morris, young teens working on James Booker Davenport's ranch on the Anglin Prong of the Sabinal River, set out on foot to find a lost ox bell. Along the way, Frank was turning cartwheels and he was very good at it. Morris tried a few times, but only achieved a clumsy imitation of Frank's skill. High above them on top of one of the steep hills that form the Sabinal Canyon five Lipan Apaches marveled at this unique method of locomotion.

Only a couple of months earlier an orphaned Frank and two of his sisters were living with their uncle Berry C. Buckelew on his Old Cedar Brake Ranch not far from the Davenport place. Uncle Berry managed Mr. Davenport's cattle as well as his own. Roundup and branding were fun activities for young Frank. On one occasion he went to Bandera City with his uncle to have their corn ground at the water-powered mill.

Purchase of coffee, cloth, and other more refined products required the long trip to San Antonio. The settlers along the Anglin Prong took turns. Berry Buckelew's turn came up in late January. With his dog Cuff by his side and his large wagon pulled by five oxen, Berry went down the Medina River gathering cypress shingles from the shingle camps along the way. About a week later, on his return trip he was ambushed and killed near Seco Creek in one of the first Kickapoo raids.

Since 1865 Kickapoo raiders were devastating the economy and lives of a region already greatly harassed by Comanches and Lipan Apaches. Over 500 Kickapoo had moved into northern Mexico during the last year of the Civil War. They had been attacked along the way by Texas militia and Confederate troops and now carried a particular grudge. They were welcomed in Mexico where they were seen as additional buffers to Comanche and Lipan Apache raids. As they consolidated their position in Mexico, they began making alliances with the various small Lipan Apache groups, organizing the raids and plunder, often having contracts in place with local Mexicans to dispose of cattle and horses.

Indians were far from the minds of Frank and Morris as they continued to clown around, enjoying the fine spring day and getting farther and farther from the ranch house. Occasionally they remembered to look for the ox bell. Suddenly some of Mr. Davenport's cattle burst out of a thicket and came running past the boys. Frank knew that stampeding cattle sometimes meant that Indians were in the country. "Looking around I thought I saw a hog, but a second glance convinced me that it was a man and an Indian, with war paint on his face, feathers in his hair, and a dirty greasy frock tail coat on his body. At this moment, he raised up with his hands high in the air, (in one he held his bow, in the other his arrows,) gave his blood-curdling war whoop and seemed to sail right at us." The boys ran. Morris was farther away from the Indian and made his escape. Frank soon found himself staring at the point of an arrow in a drawn bow.

Two more Indians emerged from the thicket and the three forced Frank up the steep hillside. At the top of the hill they led him to a point where a large flat rock jutted out over the edge. Sitting there "with an air of haughty dignity" was an older-looking Indian who stood up and began asking Frank questions in broken English. Frank, although nearly 14, gave his age as 10 because he had heard the Indians would kill rather than capture anyone much older than that. "Heap big ten year old boy," said the older Indian. "Without waiting for me to argue my case further, he very kindly and politely introduced himself to me as Custaleta [Costilietos], a war chief of the Lipan Indians."

The Indians had made saddles beforehand and stashed them in a cave along with some long lances they had brought with them. They now procured some horses and retrieved their saddles and lances. Having made a successful raid, they proceeded back to their village on the Pecos River.

Frank endured a rough initiation into the tribe. Eventually he learned to fend fairly well for himself. He hunted with bow and arrow and learned some of the Lipan language. Along with a young captive from Mexico, he was delegated to watch over the village's horse herd.

This small band of 150 Lipan Apaches made frequent moves, living a precarious existence along the Pecos River and the Rio Grande. Vigilance was maintained as their enemies included Comanches, Kickapoos, and a mysterious "tribe in blue." Scouts were sent out in relays to monitor enemy movements. Frank experienced many false alarms as the women and children scampered to the high ground while the warriors gathered their war horses and made ready for battle. "Custaleta now gave evidence of the fact that he was by far the most important figure on this occasion, the young chief and every warrior placing himself immediately under his command, the wisdom and power of this great old warchief now became evident."

As the Kickapoo were expanding their alliance, a party under Old Fox approached the village of Costilietos. Both sides arrayed for battle before a parley was made and peace concluded. Later an agent from Mexico arrived and convinced these Lipans to move into

Mexico where they would be given land and provisions in return for scouting against Comanche raiders. The Lipans were required to give up their Mexican captives. Of the six boys, three returned to their people and three chose to remain with the Lipans.

    Costilietos and his people crossed the Rio Grande and initially made camp near the town of San Vicente. They were now in contact with civilization and news of a white captive began to filter out of the region. In December 1866 J.B. Davenport heard from a friend in Eagle Pass, James Moseley, "informing me that the boy is in the hands of Kickapoo or Lipan who are encamped in the vicinity of Santa Rosa, Mexico, about 80 miles from Eagle Pass." The Texas legislature had set aside some money for the purpose of ransoming stolen children. Mr. Davenport immediately wrote to his state representative, William B. Knox, asking him to approach the governor on Frank's behalf.

    At this time W.B. Hudson was constructing a large irrigation ditch on the U.S. side of the Rio Grande. He recruited Mexican and Indian workers from the Mexican side of the border and in this manner came to know of Frank's plight. One moonlit night he sent a trusted employee to escort Frank away from his horse-herding duties. Taking two horses from the herd, the two rode across the river to the dugout house where Hudson lived with his wife and two daughters. After Frank cleaned the paint off his face and put on the suit Mrs. Hudson had made for him, he set out for Fort Clark with Mr. Hudson and the young Mexican.

    At Fort Clark Frank saw his first soldiers and learned that they wore blue uniforms. He told them about the Indians watching a tribe in blue. They were astonished because they had been in camp on the Pecos River that summer and had not seen a sign of Indians.

The trio reached the Uvalde area January 24, 1867, where County Judge Neuman Patterson sent off a letter to Governor Throckmorton asking if any of the money set aside for ransoming captives could be made available as a reward for W.B. Hudson. He felt the man deserved at least $300 for the risk he took. Indeed, the risk was considerable for Hudson eventually had to move his family to Fort Clark for protection.

Apparently doubting that money from the legislature would be forthcoming, Judge Patterson made the first of a series of contributions that the trio gathered from various ranchers along the rest of the way to Bandera City. In the traditional barter economy of the time, each rancher contributed a cow (generally considered a value of ten dollars). More than 20 Uvalde and Bandera county ranchers made contributions. Mr. Hudson could not collect his reward at that time since he was naturally concerned about the safety of his family and could not slow his return by driving a herd of cattle.

J. B. Davenport watched as three strangers rode up from the river crossing in front of his rock house on the western edge of Bandera City. Perhaps drovers looking for work, he thought, but they carried none of the usual cowboy accoutrements. One was a young Mexican, another a tough looking Anglo. The third was a young man red-faced from long exposure to the sun. Although he wore a homemade suit, his reddened face and shoulder length hair gave him the appearance of an Indian. The three strangers dismounted, opened the yard gate and stepped up to the house. The tough looking Anglo said his name was Hudson and asked Mr. Davenport if he recognized anyone in the group. He said no. But there was something about the long-haired young man as he took a closer look, then exclaimed, "I believe that's Frank Buckelew!"

Mr. Davenport took off through the town to find Frank's sisters. As he hurried amongst the townspeople (30-50 families), he spread the word that Frank was alive and home. Soon a large excited crowd was gathering around the Davenport house. A cacophony of voices rattled off questions and comments in English, German, Polish, and Spanish. Frank ran into the house and hid under a bed.

During Frank's absence, his sister, Mary, had married William Finley. Frank went to live with them on Bandera Creek. Nearby, Thomas L. Buckner taught a school that Frank attended for three months. About this time, Frank later recalled, "In the fall session of district court in Bandera county, 1867, the grand jury found a bill of kidnapping against Custaleta, et al, and fixed their bond at $5,000. The case never came to trial for lack of the appearance of the defendants."

A couple of companies of U.S. cavalry had been stationed at Camp Verde 1866-68. March 25, 1868, J.B. Davenport presided over a meeting of Bandera citizens who sent their resolutions to the general commanding the Fifth Military District. Due to the recent removal of the cavalry, the Bandera people were asking to be allowed to organize for their own defense. This, of course, was not allowed during Reconstruction.

That same year, Thomas Buckner married Frank's sister, Martha. They rented a ranch from Bill and Sam Mott. Frank went to live with them and worked as a ranch hand. As Frank recalled, "The Indians made five different raids in our settlement that summer."

That fall W.B. Hudson returned to collect his reward. He stayed a couple of days with the Buckners. Quite remarkably most of the ranchers now paid with cash. It was, perhaps, an interesting indication that many of them were profiting from the trail drives that had begun the previous year.

In 1870, when Frank was 18 years old, he married Nancy Witter. All during this time the statistics and pleas for help from a troubled region continued to pile up on bureaucratic desks at the state and federal levels until finally in 1873 President Grant sent Colonel Ranald Mackenzie and the Fourth U.S. Cavalry to Fort Clark. Colonel Mackenzie had verbal orders from his superiors to establish control of the Upper Rio Grande Border Region, an area with western points at San Felipe Del Rio and Laredo and eastern points at Bandera County and Atascosa County (south of San Antonio).

May 18, 1873, with Seminole scouts and six companies of the Fourth Cavalry, Colonel Mackenzie crossed into Mexico and destroyed one Lipan and two Kickapoo villages along the Rio San Rodrigo. Among the 40 captured Indians (mostly Kickapoo women and children) was Costilietos who had been lassoed by a Seminole scout. The Kickapoo Alliance was broken in one stroke. Subsequent negotiations by Indian commissioners convinced most of the Kickapoos to move to the Indian Territory where they could be reunited with their captive kinfolk. Lipan Apache raids, however, continued. Colonel Mackenzie found it necessary to station a company of the Fourth Cavalry in Bandera County about two miles below present day Vanderpool.

Costilietos and the other captives were held in San Antonio. While there, the old chief was allowed visits from the Tonkawa chief, Castille, and a Lipan-Tonkawa named Scout Johnson. Although Frank greatly resented his captivity, he had gained some respect and even admiration for Costilietos. He seriously considered going to visit him in San Antonio. However, there was not much time for consideration, for the news soon came that Costilietos had escaped. The <u>San Antonio Express</u> commented sarcastically July 3, 1873, "We are not informed, but suppose the military will fire a public spirited cannon. Old Costalitos should be led in triumph through the streets, but we believe we have already mentioned that he was absent." The old chief went back to leading raids into Texas. Sometime later Frank heard that he had been mortally wounded by pursuers as he was re-crossing the Rio Grande.

In 1879 Frank went to work for William Sheppard who lived with his family on the old Jack Ranch seven or eight miles north of Bandera. His recollections illustrate a mixture of seasonal activities: "That summer when the crops were laid by the men folks went to the shingle camps. They left me to guard the women in case of an Indian attack, and as no occasion presented itself to test my fighting qualities while thus entrusted, I passed for a fairly good guard. After crops were gathered we all moved to the shingle camps at the mouth of Sheppard's Creek on the Medina."

In later years Frank became a Methodist minister. His eleven months with the Indians was always in his mind, but he seldom spoke about that time until somehow he became acquainted with the anthropological team of Thomas and Lucy Dennis. In 1911, with the help of Lucy Dennis, Frank published The Life of F.M. Buckelew: The Indian Captive: As Related By Himself. In 1925 Mr. and Mrs. Dennis helped with the publication of an expanded version with the same title. J. Marvin Hunter was publishing his Pioneer History of Bandera County about that time and said, "Mr. Buckelew is an interesting character and often visits the schools of the county and relates incidents of his captivity to the school children." Francis Marion Buckelew died December 11, 1930, and was buried in the Oak Rest (or Baker) Cemetery, Medina, Texas.

Sources

Dennis, Lucy S. The Life of F.M. Buckelew: The Indian Captive: As Related By Himself. 1911.

Dennis, T.S. and Mrs. T.S. The Life of F.M. Buckelew: The Indian Captive: As Related By Himself. Hunter's Printing House. Bandera. 1925.

Denson, Mrs. Howard, Mrs. Billy Burnes and Mrs. Howard Graves. The Bandera County Cemetery Records. Bandera County Historical Survey Committee. Bandera. 197?

Hunter, J. Marvin. Pioneer History of Bandera County. Hunter's Printing House. Bandera. 1922.

Pierce, Michael D. The Most Promising Young Officer: A Life of Ranald Slidell Mackenzie. University of Oklahoma Press. Norman and London. 1993.

Robinson III, Charles M. Bad Hand: A Biography of General Ranald S. Mackenzie. State House Press. Austin. 1993.

Texas Historical Records Survey: Division of Professional and Service Projects: WPA. Inventory of the County Archives: Bandera County: No. 10. San Antonio. 1940.

Tyler, Ron, et al, eds. The New Handbook of Texas. Texas State Historical Association. Austin. 1996.

Wallace, Ernest. Ranald S. Mackenzie on the Texas Frontier. Texas A&M University Press. College Station. 1964.

Winfrey, Dorman H. and James M. Day, eds. The Indian Papers of Texas and the Southwest: 1825-1916. Pimberton Press. Austin. 1966.

Documents referenced include:

Davenport, J.B. Letter to W.B. Knox. December 22, 1866.
Oborske, E. Record of Indian Depredations In Bandera County. June 25, 1867.
(Sent to D.R. Gurley, Adjutant General of Texas).
Patterson, N.M.C. Letter to J.W. Throckmorton. January 28, 1867.

31

Sheriffs and Rangers:
Law Enforcement In Bandera County: 1866-1892

Thaddeus C. Rine

In the late summer of 1865 a company of U.S. Army troops made camp along Bandera Creek near Bandera City. The period of U.S. history known as Military Reconstruction had come to Bandera County. Throughout the defeated Confederacy the occupying U.S. Army appointed state and county officials. In these disturbed times resignations and disqualifications were common. The office of county sheriff in Bandera County is a case in point: T. C. Rine was appointed September 14, 1866 and resigned February 15, 1868. M.H. Langhfort was appointed April 25, 1868, and disqualified in June 1869. Joseph Sutherland was appointed June 23, 1869 and served until the first postwar elections December 3, 1869.

T. C. Rine won that election and served until December 2, 1873. He was born in Tennessee in 1832 and died in 1909 in San Antonio. Sheriff Rine was sometimes involved in manhunts for notorious criminals and made many arrests, but his service in office as an arbiter, diplomat, and server of papers should also be remembered.

During the early years of his tenure, more people were leaving the area than moving in. Indian raids went mostly unchecked by the U.S. Army. State militia companies were not allowed during Military Reconstruction. In Bandera County 1865-66 134 horses and mules were lost to Indian raids. In these raids, at least five men were killed and three wounded. Lipan Apaches carried young

Frank Buckelew into captivity. Total value of livestock (including cattle) stolen or killed by Indians was estimated at $7,580.00.

Most of the people in the county during these years were mainly concerned with staying alive while tending to their farms, ranches, businesses, and families. Someone might occasionally have too much to drink at George Hay's saloon, but serious legal infractions by county residents were rare. Most often, it seems, Sheriff Rine gave offenders of minor infractions a reprimand and a good-natured solicitation to vote for him in the next election. If he found it necessary to lock up anyone overnight, the prisoner was kept in his kitchen or chained to a tree. He reported only three outstanding arrest warrants for 1869. One of the warrants was for the 16 men involved in the 1863 San Julian Creek incident, carried over from term to term by subsequent Bandera County sheriffs for many years. The other two warrants were for a burglary and a theft of oxen; the suspects had left the county.

Gradually, as the 1860s gave way to the 1870s, people began moving back onto the frontier. As the cattle industry boomed, Bandera County's population increased from 399 in 1860 to 649 in 1870. Some newcomers were unsavory individuals bred in the violence and turmoil of the Civil War and the following Reconstruction; many of these already were fugitives from justice.

In 1869 Bandera County was one of 82 Texas counties with no jail. Of the total 158 counties, only 24 had jails that were reputed to be secure. With the growing climate of lawlessness in Texas, Sheriff Rine's kitchen would no longer suffice. B.F. Langford built the first jail in Bandera City with sawed 6 by 6 inch cypress timbers making a cabin 14 by 14 feet with a small opening in the top accessed by a ladder. Dangerous prisoners were chained to a metal bolt in the floor. This jail proved secure as no prisoners ever escaped from it, although some unsuccessful attempts were made from the outside to free prisoners.

County sheriffs are limited by jurisdiction and by the laws and customs of their time. The State of Texas recognized the need for law enforcement officers with statewide jurisdiction. During the Civilian Reconstruction period a Texas Ranger regiment, the Frontier Force, defended the frontiers and a State Police force attempted to curtail the growing lawlessness in the state. The Rangers were mostly involved in deterring Indian raids and were only peripherally effective as law enforcers. The State Police were largely ineffectual due to their unpopularity as enforcers of Reconstruction.

In Bandera City J.P. Heinen had built too close to the Medina River and lost his general store in the 1870 flood. He was getting by on carpentry work when he accepted the appointment to the State Police for Bandera County. His recollection of that time:

> There were many bad men on the frontier in those days, generally in sparsely settled regions where they thought they could do as they pleased. To arrest and bring to trial these criminals was the purpose of the organization of the state police. From one to three men in each county were appointed on the force. I was the only one in Bandera county, and I served two years, resigning at the end of the second year. The pay was $60 per month, and we had to furnish our own equipment, horses, arms, etc. The pay was wholly inadequate considering the risks we were constantly called upon to face.

The times were likely worse to the south in neighboring Medina County where there were no State Police officers. Perhaps the passage of the San Antonio-El Paso Road through the county funneled more of the rougher element into that region. Medina County rancher and

Texas Ranger, H.J. Richarz, wrote to the governor asking that State Police be appointed for Medina County. The area around D'Hanis, he said, was particularly overrun with murderers and rustlers.

Republicans were out in the next election. T.C. Rine eventually moved his family to San Antonio where he served on the police force. He maintained a ranch in Bandera County and family members often spent their summers there.

Henry Hamilton

J.B. Davenport was elected sheriff December 2, 1873 and resigned April 12, 1874. C.H. Frick was elected May 16, 1874 and served through February 15, 1876. Henry "Buck" Hamilton won that election as well as the next five.

Buck Hamilton married Anne Phillips in Tennessee in 1856 and they moved to Kerr County in 1859. A farmer, rancher, trail boss, and entrepreneur, Buck Hamilton was Kerr County Sheriff 1862-64. In 1869 he moved his family to Bandera City where he established the Bandera Hotel and a stage line between Bandera and San Antonio. He was elected sheriff of Bandera County in 1876 and served until 1888.

Sheriff Hamilton's brother-in-law, Jackson Phillips, had a ranch on Winan's Creek six miles from Bandera City. He was captain of a minuteman ranger company that disbanded around 1874 or '75. He had been Buck Hamilton's deputy sheriff for less that a year when on the way to Sabinal Canyon he was attacked and killed by Indians at Seco Pass.

The December 1876 raid in which Jack Phillips was killed caused a great deal of consternation among the settlements, but was probably the last Comanche raid through the region. Lipan Apaches continued to raid in western Bandera and Kerr counties, but the time of Indian raids was almost over. The Frontier Battalion of Texas Rangers had formed in 1874 and ranger patrols covered as much of the Indian raiding routes as possible. U.S. Army campaigns under Colonel Ranald Mackenzie ravaged the home bases of Indian raiders in Mexico and on the Panhandle plains. Furthermore, the buffalo were quickly disappearing.

In March 1877, the adjutant general of Texas ordered the Frontier Battalion to cease regular Indian patrols unless in actual pursuit. Control of lawlessness became a priority as detachments of rangers went riding out to scour the frontier. August 16, 1877, Major John B. Jones, commanding the battalion, wrote to Adjutant General Steele:

> I learn from one of my men just in from Frio that Capt. Coldwell started on ten days scout to Bandera County on the 12th inst. Had two other Scouts out at same time in different directions all for ten days and only three men in camp when my informant left.

In the August heat Captain Neal Coldwell and three rangers from Company A rode into Bandera City. The three were John Parker, Hawk Roberts, and James B. Gillett. Ranger Gillett later wrote an account of their week in Bandera County. The rangers went out in pairs and soon filled the Bandera County jail with 10-12 fugitives from justice, illustrating the appropriateness of the title of Frederick Wilkins' history of Texas Rangers: <u>The Law Comes To Texas</u>.

One of the fugitives was wanted for murder in Burnet County. He had recently stood off a Bandera County deputy sheriff. Ranger Gillet said that Captain Coldwell instructed Hawk Roberts and him to "take no chances with this man—this meant to kill him if he hesitated about surrendering." Sheriff Hamilton gave them a guide to the fugitive's hideout, about 15 miles northwest of Bandera City. It was near dark when the guide pointed out the house and hurried back to town. The two rangers waited for dawn. At daylight they stepped quietly into the house where they found the man asleep on a pallet. Hawk Roberts kicked a white-handled .45 pistol away and the fugitive woke to find two Winchester rifles in his face. As James Gillet remembered:

> Of course he surrendered without a fight. His wife, who was sleeping in a bed in the same room, jumped out of it and heaped all kinds of abuse on us for entering her home without ceremony. She was especially bitter against Sheriff Hamilton, who, she said, had promised to notify her husband when he was wanted so he could come in and give himself up. She indignantly advised her husband to give old sheriff Hamilton a damned good whipping the first chance he had.

John King Fisher was a notorious Uvalde County rancher who was sometimes an outlaw and sometimes a lawman. July 29, 1877, Lieutenant J.L. Hall had reported from Castroville that Sergeant Parrott was in camp with 18 rangers just returned with King Fisher in custody after having scouted all over Uvalde, Bandera, Maverick, Medina, and Atascosa counties. King Fisher was captured several times by Texas Rangers, but never convicted in the courts. On one of his law-abiding occasions he was driving some cattle up the trail, passing through Bandera County, and stayed for dinner at the Maverick ranch. Mrs. Maverick remembered that she had a nice conversation with him about his wife and children before she knew who he was. He was running for Uvalde County sheriff when he was killed in a San Antonio gunfight March 11, 1884.

By 1880 Bandera County's population had reached 2,158. The county was still using the old Schmidtke & Hay building as a courthouse and more space was needed. At the same time the cypress wood jail seemed inadequate. The esteemed architect Alfred Giles designed a new jail for Bandera County and James A. Courtney constructed the stone building in 1881. It included offices for county officials. During Sheriff Hamilton's tenure, no one escaped from this jail.

Buck Hamilton's sense of fair play may be illustrated in an incident remembered by Robert Maudslay: By the late 1870s railroads passed to the north and south of Bandera County. U.S. railroads widely advertised the availability of land along their routes and attracted many immigrants from the British Isles. Among them were Robert and Harry Maudslay who staked a homestead on some unoccupied land next to the land they had bought in Bandera County. Their mother and three sisters established a girls' school in Bandera City.

The Maudslay brothers encountered a challenge to their homestead from a claim jumper. Although the dispute was eventually settled peacefully in court, the brothers from England experienced some Wild West excitement before it was done. After a heated incident between the claim jumper and Harry Maudslay, Sheriff Buck Hamilton came by the Maudslay place and asked Harry if he carried a gun. Robert Maudslay recalled, "On being told that he didn't, the sheriff said, 'Then take this one; I think you're going to need it.' Whereupon he gave Harry a .38 calibre pistol with all its chambers loaded."

After another close encounter, Sheriff Hamilton visited the Maudslay ranch again as Robert Maudslay continued, "After this incident, I was also presented with a pistol, and thereafter I might be seen following my peaceful occupation of plowing with a six-shooter partly exposed from my hip pocket. I practiced with it a little, too, and sometimes came quite near to hitting what I shot at."

The event that revealed the sliver of land the Maudslay brothers homesteaded was a flurry of surveying activity necessitated by the coming of barbed wire fencing to Bandera County. The landscape and the way of life on open range began to change extremely. Sometimes in the early days of fencing, common roads were fenced across and some landholders were cut off from water. The Big Pasture men, the large landholders who favored fencing, faced off against the fence-cutters who were often smaller landholders and included some cattlemen who owned no land and others who opposed fencing for various reasons. Eventually water rights were worked out and new laws required gates on common roads, but before it was all over, some counties had to call in Texas Rangers to restore order. While no record has been found that Rangers were needed in Bandera County, a fall 1883 edition of the Bandera <u>Enterprise</u> editorialized:

> It appears to us that it is high time some effective steps were being taken to settle the troubles between the pasture men and their enemies. Considerable blood has already been shed, and dangerous sentiments are rapidly assuming such proportions as to become a rational source of alarm.

That the Rangers were not needed again in Bandera County after 1877 is probably a tribute to Sheriff Hamilton and his deputies. Among the men who served as deputy sheriffs for Buck Hamilton were John Pyka, Bladen Mitchell, Henry S. Hudspeth, and F.J. McCarthy.

In late July 1888 Buck Hamilton fell ill with a serious case of measles. He seemed to recover, then relapsed and died. Bandera had two newspapers at that time: The July 26 edition of the <u>Enterprise</u> eulogized, "not only a good officer, but...a good man...whose large and generous soul was a well-spring of cheerful good humor." The <u>Bugle</u> concurred, "Necessarily his sheriffship made him widely known, and he will be long remembered for his fund of anecdote, his practical jokes, his kindly disposition, and for the many good deeds done without ostentation and in secret." He was 55 years old and had been Bandera County sheriff for 12 years.

H.S. Hudspeth was appointed sheriff August 1, 1888, serving through November 6, 1888, when Valerius P. Sanders was elected.

V.P. Sanders (sometimes seen as Saunders)

Valerius Palentine Sanders was born in Tennessee, September 1833. He was still a small child when his family moved to Texas. He was 21 in Cibolo in 1855 when he enlisted as a private in Callahan's Mounted Rangers. He was among those who fought at Escondido when Captain Callahan took his men into Mexico. Through 1858-59 he was again a Texas Ranger, serving under John S. Ford. Captain Ford led 102 rangers coordinated with Captain S.P. Ross and 100 Indian volunteers from the Brazos Reservation. They ventured deep into the Comanche plains and attacked the village of Iron Jacket.

When the Civil War began, V.P. Sanders was in Hood County where he enrolled in the 15th Regiment, Texas Cavalry, under Colonel George H. Sweet. He began service as captain of Company A, but was soon promoted to the rank of major. The regiment served west of the Mississippi River until surrendered in the Battle of Arkansas Post on January 11, 1863. The regiment was exchanged April 1863, and served east of the Mississippi thereafter.

The men were dismounted at Little Rock, Arkansas, and consolidated with other depleted regiments to form the 32nd Texas Cavalry, Grandbury's Brigade, Cleburne"s Division, Hardee's Corps, Army of Tennessee. Major Sanders lost his right arm November 11, 1863, at Tunnel Hill, Tennessee, in the fighting leading up to the Battle of Chattanooga. [Coincidentally, 3rd Corporal John Hardin, serving in the same regiment, lost his right arm September 1, 1864, in the fighting around the Siege of Atlanta, at Jonesborough, Georgia.]

The 1870 census found the former soldier in Harrison (Franklin County), Kansas, with an occupation of cattle dealer. He was in Bandera County for the 1880 census which states his occupation as a sheep raiser. Apparently, he employed William Edwards as a servant. Edwards lived in the same household along with his wife, Elizabeth, and two children, John and Lue.

Major V.P. Sanders served two terms as Bandera County Sheriff 1888-1892. The 1900 census shows that he held the office of county treasurer and boarded at Hugh Duffy's Bandera Hotel. At some point, he was the county's postmaster. He was 75 when he died in Uvalde December 31, 1908.

Sources

Baenziger, Ann Patton. "The Texas State Police During Reconstruction: A Reexamination." <u>The Southwestern Historical Quarterly</u>. Volume 72. Number 4. (April 1969) Pages 470-491.

Burnside, Sabrina Rine. "Recollections of Sabrina Rine Burnside." <u>Bandera County Historian</u>. Volume 10. Number 1. (Spring 1987) Pages 1-6.

Fifteenth Texas Cavalry. Texans in the Civil War. Texansinthecivilwar.com/15th _Calvary/. (Accessed 11 13 10)

Gard, Wayne. "The Fence-Cutters." The Southwestern Historical Quarterly. Volume 51. Number One. (July 1947) Pages 1-15.

Gardner, Amanda. "King of the Road." Texas Highways. Volume 45. Number 12. (December 1998) Pages 38-42.

Gillett, James B. Six Years With The Texas Rangers. Von Boeckmann-Jones Company. Austin. 1921. (Incidentally he remembered the Bandera County sheriff as "Jack Hamilton." He may have confused the sheriff's name with that of a county commissioner of the time named Jack Hamilton).

Greenwood, John M. Biographs of Family Ancestors. Sons of Confederate Veterans. Author's Collection.

Hall, J.L., Lieutenant. Report to William Steele. July 29, 1877. Adjutant General Records. Archives Division. Texas State Library. Austin.

Hunter, J. Marvin. The Pioneer History of Bandera County. Hunter's Printing House. Bandera. 1922.

Hunter, J. Marvin. 100 Years In Bandera: 1853-1953. The Bandera Bulletin. Bandera. 1953.

Jones, John B., Major. Report to William Steele. August 16, 1877. Adjutant General Records. Archives Division. Texas State Library. Austin.

Loth, Donna Schultke. Geneological Research on V.P. Sanders. Bandera County Genweb Site.

Maudslay, Robert. Texas Sheepman. University of Texas Press. Austin. 1951.

McKay, Scott. "Casualties of the 6th, 10th, and 15th Consolidated Regiment at Tunnel Hill, Tennessee,

November 25, 1863." Armoryguards.org. (Accessed 11 04 10.)

Muster Roll. Callahan's Mounted Rangers. 1855. Archives Division. Texas State Library. Austin.

Muster Roll Extracts: V.P. Sanders, Ford's 2nd Company. Archives Division. Texas State Library. Austin.

Richarz, H.J., Captain. Letter to Edmund J. Davis. December 29, 1870. Governor's Records. Archives Division. Texas State Library. Austin.

Rine, T.C. Report of Outstanding Bandera County Arrest Warrants. August 3, 1870. Governor's Records. Archives Division. Texas State Library. Austin.

Rodriguez, Jose Policarpo. Jose Policarpo Rodriguez: "The Old Guide": Surveyor, Scout, Hunter, Indian Fighter, Ranchman, Preacher: His Life in His Own Words. Publishing House of the Methodist Episcopal Church, South. Nashville and Dallas. 1898?

Stevens, Tom M. "A Bandera County Minute Man." Frontier Times. Volume 3. Number 4. (January 1926) Pages 21-22.

Sowell, A.J. Early Settlers and Indian Fighters of Southwest Texas: Facts Gathered From Survivors of Frontier Days. Ben C. Jones & Co. Austin. 1900.

Texas Historical Records Survey: Division of Professional and Service Projects: WPA. Inventory of the County Archives: Bandera County: No. 10. San Antonio. 1940.

Tise, Sammy. Texas County Sheriffs. Oakwood Printing. Albuquerque. 1989.

U.S. Census 1860, '70, and '80. U.S. Census Bureau. United States Historical Census Data Browser. Fisher.lib.virginia.edu/census/. ICPSR.

Wilkins, Frederick. The Law Comes To Texas: The Texas Rangers: 1870-1901. State House Press. Austin. 1999.

Winfrey, Dorman H. and James M. Day, eds. The Indian Papers of Texas and the Southwest: 1825-1916. Pimberton Press. Austin. 1966. Five Volumes.

Wilkins, Frederick. Defending The Borders: The Texas Rangers 1848-1861. State House Press. Austin. 2001.

The first jail in Bandera City, which J. Marvin Hunter described in 100 Years In Bandera:

It consisted of a small room about 14x14 feet made of sawed cypress timbers, 6x6 inches in thickness, laid flat one on top of another. Only one small window, placed near the top, afforded light and ventilation. There was no door, only an opening in the flat roof, fitted with a lid. A ladder led to the top of the little square building. Prisoners were taken up on this ladder, then the ladder was pulled up and used to put the prisoner down inside the jail. A ring was bolted to the floor, and desperate prisoners were chained to this ring to prevent escape. This is one jail no prisoner ever escaped from, although one or two attempts were made by friends on the outside to release a prisoner.

32

The Life Story of
Mrs. Annie E. Brown Revisited

> While here Grandpa Cazey came and begged me to leave; said he was afraid he would have to come and pick up my bones some day. I replied that if it was to be my fate I would just as soon have him pick them up as anybody, but this was my home and I intended to stay.

One of the most compelling stories in Marvin Hunter's **Pioneer History of Bandera County** is the account of Mrs. Annie E. Brown. Born among the well-to-do of La Fourche Parish, Louisiana, near Thibadeauxville in 1838, she was orphaned at an early age and raised by a guardian on a nearby plantation. Under private tutors, she learned arithmetic, spelling, writing, and reading, as well as English, French, and Latin.

At the age of 18, she received her inheritance and went to live with relatives near Alexandria, Louisiana. Here she met a young wholesale clerk and they were married November 25, 1859. On the eve of the Civil War they decided to move to California and so set out for Austin, Texas, where they expected to meet up with an immigrant train. They had sold all their property in Louisiana and traveled in "a light spring wagon."

The account is not very clear on the timeframe, but apparently the war had already broken out when they reached Austin. They found there were no wagon trains leaving for California and news of Indian raids made their solitary journey unthinkable. Instead they attempted to reach California by way of Mexico, learned that they could not cross into Mexico unless they were selling cotton, and then learned they could not cross even so. By this time Mrs. Brown was expecting her first child. Near Castroville, she first boarded with a family named Beipert, then rented a room from Christian Santleben whose son, August, had just finished a year as Bandera's first mail carrier. Mr. Brown engaged in the cotton freighting business on the road between San Antonio and Eagle Pass.

The timeframe remains foggy, but 1862 passed by (for Sibley's Brigade is mentioned) and Mr. Brown continued freighting under various circumstances. It may have been when the war ended that the Browns turned to farming on rented land around Castroville. They had little success and moved to the area around present-day Devine where they "'squatted' on a piece of land about two miles from that place." Life was hard and Indian raids proved worrisome, but the Browns found Big Foot Wallace "to be an excellent neighbor." The farm, however, was not making it and whatever money they had brought with them from Louisiana was long gone. Mr. Brown went to San Antonio and then to Fort Worth to look for work. He died of an illness before he could return. Mrs. Brown became a single parent with two small children to raise.

She had learned something about the freighting business and sold or traded the "improvements" on her land to Captain Wallace to start a one wagon freighting company. The young black man she hired to do the freighting quit the job when he got married and the resourceful Mrs. Brown then opened a boarding house with Big Foot Wallace as one of the boarders. This business was a success, but after some years, when Mrs. Brown attempted to expand her enterprise into cotton farming, a drought set her back some.

A neighbor had moved to Bandera County and "came back and gave me such a glowing description of the cool, full flowing streams, fine grass and picturesque mountains, that I decided to come here." She gives the date as November 25, 1876, when some neighbors helped her with the move. They spent a freezing night camped at Barnes Bluff, near present-day Tarpley. She stayed with the Lewis family until spring arrived. While there she heard the news of the county's last Comanche raid and the killing of Deputy Sheriff Phillips on nearby Seco Creek. People in the area were still jittery about the raid when Mrs. Brown said, "having filed on land as a homestead, I felt that I should go and live on it, as the law required it, and, over the protest of my neighbors, I took my son and camped under a large oak tree." Grandpa Cazey came by and begged her to leave, but she would not.

Surprisingly, Mrs. Brown was only one of 22 women who filed homestead claims in Bandera County between 1870 and 1898. Of the 59 counties in the Bexar Land District, only Atascosa County had more women claimants with 32. Bexar and Hartley counties tied for third with 17 each. The number of woman claimants in the remaining counties ranged between one and 15, with the average for the district at around 5.4 per county.

After a summer of camping on her homestead, Mrs. Brown left to dispose of her property in the Devine area. When she returned, she found that her Hondo Canyon neighbors had erected a log cabin for her. It still lacked a roof so she spent three months living at a neighbor's while she taught nine pupils. "Most of the neighbors paid tuition in trade or work. Mr. Hudspeth paid money, and Jim Lewis paid me with shingles with which I covered my house and the next spring I moved back to it."

In various trading deals she had acquired a couple of cows and their calves and began building a herd. It would be some time before she could make a viable living from cattle raising. About this time the Maverick family bought the Mott Ranch and Mrs. Brown spent three years as their house manager. Gradually this led her into the profession of nursing as she went to San Antonio with the Mavericks when they sold their ranch.

The nursing profession was still young and many readers will remember the pioneering work of Clara Barton and Florence Nightingale had begun only in the preceding decades. Mrs. Brown was very careful to state, "I always nursed under specific directions of a doctor." Indeed, she worked with some of the most avant-garde medical men in the state. She remembered Doctor Cupples, the Herff brothers, and a half dozen other doctors with whom she worked.

George Cupples, Scottish born, came to Texas with the Castro Colony, and served as president of the Bexar County Medical Society and later the Texas Medical Association as well as serving as delegate to many national and international medical conventions.

German born Ferdinand Herff helped organize the Bexar County Medical Society, the Texas Medical Association, other medical organizations, and the first hospital in San Antonio. He was probably the most renowned surgeon in the state in his time. His brother, Adolf Herff, was also a well known physician.

Around 1889, President Benjamin Harrison appointed San Antonio businessman and Republican Party official, Edwin H. Terrell, to be ambassador to Belgium. The Terrell family traveled to Europe with Mrs. Annie E. Brown as their governess and family nurse. When Ambassador Terrell was transferred to Russia, Mrs. Brown decided it was time to return to Texas. She spent some years nursing around the state and in Mexico, before finally settling down on her homestead again.

Apparently her son had remained on the homestead managing the greatly increased cattle. She expanded her property from the original 160 acres to 480 and did well in the cattle business. However, in 1916, her son wanted to move to Arizona and they sold most of the cattle to give him a start there. She continued farming for some time, but around 1920 sold her original homestead for a comfortable price and settled back to enjoy her remaining years. As she told Mrs. L. Hicks of Tarpley, "I live alone from choice, that I may feel free to work when I please, play or read whenever I wish, and do as I like." She was around 84 years old when her story appeared in the Pioneer History. Mrs. Annie E. Brown died September 8, 1927, and is buried in the Tarpley Cemetery.

Sources

Denson, Mrs. Howard, Mrs. Billy Burnes and Mrs. Howard Graves. The Bandera County Cemetery Book. Bandera County Historical Survey Committee. Bandera. 197?

Gould, Florence C. and Patricia N. Pando. Claiming Their Land: Women Homesteaders In Texas. Texas Western Press. El Paso. 1991.

Hunter, J. Marvin. **The Pioneer History of Bandera County.** Hunter's Publishing House. Bandera. 1922. [The University of North Texas Library: **http://texashistory.unt.edu/data/TBDP/UNT/metapth-27720.tkl** to the Pioneer History, title page. Directly to The Life Story of Mrs. Annie E. Brown: **http://texashistory.unt.edu/ark:/67531/metapth277**

20/m128/?q=The Life Story of Mrs. Annie E. Brown]

Tyler, Ron, et al, eds. The New Handbook of Texas. Texas State Historical Association. Austin. 1996. **http://www.tsha.utexas.edu/handbook/online/**

33

Terror In The Afternoon: The 1881 Frio Canyon Raid

By the late 1870s Bandera County east of the Frio/Sabinal divide was fairly well settled. Some second and third generations of the settlers of Bandera and Medina counties moved to the Frio Canyon, the area of western Bandera County that later became Real County. John Leakey and a few other intrepid settlers had established the town of Leakey on the Frio River. Irrigation projects and available land made the area inviting to farmers, but the Frio Water Hole at the head of the river was a magnet to Indian raiders and very few people settled north of Leakey. To the west some settlement had begun along the upper Nueces River and efforts had been made to organize the region into Edwards County.

The McLaurens were among Texans looking for new land and found it in the Frio Canyon. John M. McLauren was born around 1848 in North Carolina and had come to Texas around 1857. Catherine "Kate" Ringer was born in Alabama around 1850 and married John in 1871 in Lockhart, Caldwell County. In the mid- to-late 1870s, they settled with their young children about two miles south of Leakey. John's younger brother, William, was born in North Carolina in 1853 and also settled in the Frio Canyon.

In the late 1870s the frequency of Indian raids in Texas diminished considerably. One of the last Comanche raids into the Bandera region took place in 1876. Nevertheless, in 1879, Victorio and the Mescalero Apaches were making news in far West Texas and Lipan Apaches made at least two raids around Bandera County. In the surrounding area, a woman and two children were killed in the Nueces Canyon and, in another raid, some children in Kerr County. The activities of the rangers from Camp Wood and the soldiers of Fort Clark helped calm settlers' fears. A Texas Ranger company was moved into Kerr County where one ranger remembered his time there as quiet. It seemed the days of the Indian raids might be over. In 1880 John McLauren decided to risk moving out beyond the currently settled area to establish a farm about seven miles north of Leakey.

The new McLauren place nestled beneath high rock bluffs along the Frio River. The family was doing well enough to hire a 14-year-old boy, Allen Lease, to help with the chores. They could also afford to board their oldest daughter, Mary (8), with the Richard Humphrey family in order for her to attend school in Leakey.

The morning of Tuesday, April 19, 1881, began without portent. Mr. McLauren left early on horseback to buy supplies at the store in "The Ditch" (later Rio Frio). The younger children, Maud (6), Alonzo (3), and William Frank (1) were all about as Mrs. McLauren and Allen finished up morning chores around the house, and then had dinner. Allen's birthday was coming up the next day, but there is no mention in the accounts if he had special plans. Perhaps it was a topic of conversation while they ate.

After dinner, Kate took the children out to the garden about 60 yards from the house. As Allen and Kate set to work, a rancher named John Thompson rode by within waving distance and moved on down the canyon. Some time later Kate needed a rest and the baby needed nursing, so she sat down on a blanket she had brought for that purpose. Alonzo and Maud were also on the blanket. About that time Kate heard some noises around the house and thought the hogs were tearing into something. She sent Allen to chase the hogs away from the house. He began to run over. It was about two o'clock and Allen Lease would not live to celebrate his 15th birthday and the newspaper would not even get his name right. Friday, April 22, the San Antonio <u>Daily Express</u> printed a vague report from Uvalde:

Mysterious Triple Murder: Mysterious Mob Kill Three Persons in Edwards County--McLaurence and Wife and a Mr. Case.

Special to the San Antonio Express.

> Uvalde, Texas, April 21st, 1881.-On last Tuesday afternoon, a party of fifteen men rode up to the McLaurence's house, on the Frio, in Edwards county, and took the lives of McLaurence, his wife and a young man living with them, named Case. The whole affair is shrouded in mystery, as everything pertaining to the household was left undisturbed. The above news was brought here this afternoon by parties living in that neighborhood. The particulars have not yet been received.

[The report of John McLauren's death proved premature when the paper received the particulars in time for its April 24th edition:]

The McLaurin Ranch Tragedy
    Another Account of the Frio Canon Horror

Special Correspondence San Antonio Express

> Rio Frio, Texas April 20.-On yesterday about 40 Indians visited the upper part of this canon, fifteen miles above this point, and killed Mrs. John McLaurin and Allen Reiss, of Uvalde, while in the garden near the house at work. When they discovered the Indians, Mr. Reiss started to the house to get his gun, but was shot down before he could reach it.

Terror In The Afternoon: The 1881 Frio Canyon Raid

Mrs. McLaurin started to run for [her] life and was shot down also.

Her three little children were with her, and the oldest, six or seven years old, "Little Maud," when her mamma fell, ran to the house, and taking a pillow from the bed placed it under the lady's head and then placed the two small children by her side, and started for G.W. Fisher's house to give the alarm.

Little Maud says when she was in the house after the pillow, that it was full of men, "big black men". They did not seem to take any notice of the child. They destroyed everything in the house of any value, even the sewing machine.

There will be a party of men leave here to-day in pursuit, but with very little prospects of overtaking the murderers.

Mr. D.W. Ward and wife were in the vicinity looking at the country, and have not been heard from. Fears are entertained for their safety. Everybody is greatly excited over the sad affair.

The weather is dry, with very high winds. The crops are in good condition but will need rain in a short time.

L.C. Neel

A.J. Sowell's account got the year wrong (1882), but agrees, in most of the particulars, with the April 24th newspaper account: Allen abruptly stopped running when he saw Indians in and around the house. He had turned to run back towards the garden when he was shot in the back of the head. He fell forward dead. As Mrs. Charles M. Harpole of San Antonio in 1924, Maud was not sure if Allen had actually seen the Indians or had just turned around to close the garden gate when he was shot.

In the A.J. Sowell account, Kate McLauren jumped up with the baby in her arms and told Maud and Alonzo to run for the fence along the river. At that moment an Indian at the house fired his Winchester and hit Kate in the chest. The same Indian kept firing as she somehow struggled to her feet. She was hit in her right arm as she desperately ran towards the fence. Before reaching it, she was wounded twice in the right leg and once in the hip. At the fence she handed the baby over to Maud, but was shot once more through the hip. She could not get over the fence and collapsed there. Maud's 1924 recollection was that her mother had first been shot in the hip and received four more gunshot wounds at the fence.

Maud saw her mother writhing on the ground in pain. Her six-year-old mind decided that the thing to do would be to get a pillow from the house so her mother could be more comfortable. She ran through the garden, past Allen's body, and into the house then being ransacked by Lipan Apaches. They were breaking up the place, "even the sewing machine," as the newspaper said. Maud stepped among them, retrieved a pillow, and hurried back to her mother without incident.   In her 1924 interview, Maud did not mention the pillow, but said only, "When the Indians left, I went to the house and brought a dipper of water for her."

In the A.J. Sowell account, with the pillow now under her head, Kate told Maud to run for help to George Fisher who lived about a mile down the river. Maud sat Alonzo and Frank beside their mother and hurried off as she was told. She found him fishing along the river and told him what had happened. Mr. Fisher carried the breathless girl up to his house and set out to alert his nearest neighbors, James Hicks, Henry Wall, and Mrs. Goodman. Maud and Mrs. Goodman were then taken to David Thompson's house while the men went out to gather a force to fight the Indians. Mrs. Goodman's appeal to go directly to Kate McLauren's aid was voted down.

James Hicks went down river to John Leakey, an old Indian fighter, who gathered a couple of his Mexican employees and set out on foot for the McLauren place. John McLauren, on his way back home, caught up with Leakey and, as they passed J.B. Johnson's place, George Fisher joined them. They reached Kate shortly before sundown. She weakly asked for water, which her husband brought up from the river in his hat brim. She drank some, but was dead within a few more minutes. The Indians, perhaps fifteen in number, were long gone.

The following day sixteen men gathered to go after the raiders. Some of their fathers had done the same thing in the earlier days of settlement in Bandera, Medina, or Uvalde counties. W.J. McLauren was captain according to Sowell's account. Tobe Edwards was 17 at the time and later related that the men who gathered were part of a county minuteman ranger company under the command of Lieutenant John Avant who was away at the time. Sowell also lists James Hicks, [Thomas?] Coryell, H.T. Coston, Henry "Boy" Wall, Frank Pollard, George Leakey, M.V. Pruitt, John Thompson, and Frank Sanders. Edwards' account adds the name of Hugh Colton. The Sowell account includes the disclaimer that John McLauren remained behind due to eye injuries he had received the day before. Apparently in his hurry to get home, he rode his horse into a tree branch.

The trail was followed up the bluffs above the house and west as far as Kickapoo Springs near the head of the West Fork of the Nueces River, but many of the horses were giving out and most of the men turned back. William McLauren, Tobe Edwards, H.T. Coston, and Coryell pressed on. At the Nueces River Nick Colton, Sam Rainey, Jim Waldy and his brother joined them. They reached the slopes of the Rio Grande Valley where they waited while Coryell turned south to Fort Clark. He informed the army of the raid and the location of the raiders' trail.

According to the U.S. Army report, Lieutenant John L. Bullis and thirty Seminole-Negro scouts from Fort Clark followed the raiders' trail for six days into the Sierra del Burros of Mexico. On the evening of May 3, 1881, they surrounded the raiders' camp and attacked at dawn. Four Indians were reported killed and a woman and child were taken prisoner.

In the A.J. Sowell account, "A general charge was now made on the camp, and some were killed before they got up from where they were lying, and others as they ran." Five Indians were killed in this account and some who escaped were wounded. The captured woman, wounded in one hand, admitted being on the raid and said that she had prevented the men from killing the children. John McLauren made a trip to Fort Clark and identified some objects taken from his home.

According to Tobe Edwards, there were seven men in the raiding party and he stated that Bullis and his men killed six. He said the Indian woman stated that this group had gone on raids to the region of the Frio Water Hole every month for 20 years. Edwards and the others had been on the trail for 13 ½ days. Ten days later they heard the results from Bullis.

The bodies of Catherine McLauren and Allen Lease were taken down to Leakey where their burials were the first in the Florel-Leakey Cemetery. Their gravesites are a short distance diagonally apart.

Sources

Early Settlers and Indian Fighters of Southwest Texas.

The New Handbook of Texas.

The Old Army In Texas.

The Pioneer History of Bandera County.

The San Antonio Daily Express.

Six Years With The Texas Rangers.

1880 U.S. Census.   Bandera County (4th Precinct)

Edwards County

34

The Maudslay Academy

Ellen Maudslay, a fifty-six-year-old widow with her children in their 20s, came from Manchester, England. They took the train from New York to San Antonio in August 1882. Mrs. Maudslay stepped into the steamy midday air and onto the platform with her four daughters Louise, Amy, Ada, and Alice and youngest son, Robert. They were met by the elder son, Harry, who had come ahead of them to purchase land.

They set out for Bandera City in a horse carriage, camping the first night on Red Bluff Creek. Robert remembered, "After living practically all our lives in a great city and becoming accustomed to its noise, we found the first night in the woods almost painful in its silence. But it passed, and we were on our way again early the next morning, arriving at our new home long before the sun went down."

There was still much of the frontier feeling to the region. The previous year Kate McLauren and Allen Lease had been killed by Indians on the Frio River (the far western portion of Bandera County at that time). A couple of years earlier Arthur Pue and an assailant killed each other in a gunfight outside a Bandera saloon. The range was still open and it would be another year or two before barbed wire began to appear around some of the larger ranches. It was the height of the cattle boom years and Bandera City was a rough, bustling, and busy place.

At the same time late Nineteenth Century social trends from across the nation filtered into the region. Women became more involved in public life through their church groups and other organizations. A Catholic church had been established with the first Polish settlers. Gradually other denominations in the county included Methodist, Baptist, Episcopalian, and Later Day Saints (although all did not have their own church building). A branch of the United Friends of Temperance had organized in Bandera City in 1879 with 13 men and 20 women.

Railroad companies widely advertised the virtues of the lands their trains could take people to. The British Isles were frequent targets of that advertising and often some individuals, and families like the Maudslays and the Guthries, arrived in the county with high hopes and greenhorn enthusiasm.

In 1880 John Alexander Guthrie brought his family from Scotland. His attempt at ranching failed, but he had been raised in the newspaper business. He bought the <u>Bandera Bugle</u>, giving the county a paper in the latest journalistic style complete with wire reports. He dabbled in real estate and, with Doctor George H. Rice, published a pamphlet extolling the land, merchants, industries, and healthful atmosphere of Bandera City and County. Mr. Guthrie described the town:

> Within its boundaries it contains four stores, lumber yard, two blacksmith shops, two carpenters, a saddler, three druggists, three house builders, two butchers, one surgeon, a catholic chapel and school taught by Sisters of Charity, a Methodist church, and a large school house, one saloon, a court house and jail, two large and fully equipped hotels, There is also one saw and two grist and flour mills, two cotton gins, two worked by water and one by steam and two weekly newspapers published, the <u>Bugle</u>, the county paper and the Enterprise.
>
> The city is laid out in lots, and these can be obtained at from $40 to $80 each. Outside of the

city there is no vacant land in large bodies, but there are a number of desirable farms for sale.

Doctor Rice wrote his medical assessment of the county in the pamphlet. His newspaper ad stated that he specialized in women's conditions. An article reports that he ran a 50-yard dash with another of the town's doctors as part of the frivolities at the weekly horse races that were held along San Julian Creek. In 1891 the athletic doctor captained Bandera's first baseball team.

Harry Maudslay had bought the family a small ranch near town. He had built a house on a hill overlooking Bandera Creek. Robert humorously recalled all the buckets of water they had to carry up the hill from the creek, their only source of water. They lacked proper farm implements and the field they cleared for corn was dotted with tree stumps. They tried raising cattle on land that was unsuitable for that purpose, but later had better luck raising horses. Many of which they entered in the local races.

However the men fared at ranching and farming, the women of the family had assets of their own. According to Charles Ramsdell, "These daughters had been educated at the very best schools available to young English women in those days, and the thoroughness of their preparation was amazing." Furthermore, they had teaching experience at an English prep school, Cheetham Collegiate School.

When a piano bought in New York arrived, Mrs Maudslay, with Louise, Amy, and Ada, moved to a residence at the corner of Eleventh and Hackberry streets in Bandera City. Here they opened the Maudslay Academy, A Select School For Young Ladies. Teenage girls, that is, and the first three were Maud Ellis, Mary Guthrie, and Ella Langford. Small boys were also taught in a separate operation. Alice remained on the ranch where she taught a private school.

Robert Maudslay wrote letters to their relatives in England, relating experiences of their new life. In later years his niece, Winifred Kupper, set them down in a book. He said of the Academy:

> From what we gathered, the Maudslay School did a good job with French, music, drawing, literature—mostly English—and mathematics, but when it came to history it seems that the American story was largely neglected in favor of a thorough knowledge of the British rulers from the first to Victoria. The Civil War in America your aunts knew little of, and as far as the American Revolution it was passed off as an unimportant squabble with a bunch of rather barbaric colonists.

Ramsdell also noted the British slant on history, "When they reached the American Revolution the girls were somewhat surprised to learn that the British had not much wanted to keep America, anyhow." Nevertheless, the courses were rigorous. Academy alumna Adah Gibbons recalled,

> "Both place geography and simple geography were taught. The former included elaborate map drawing and the latter the rudiments of physics—of course, without benefit of laboratory.
>
> The young ladies were given stiff courses in history and literature. In English history they were required to name all the kings, the dates of their reigns, and the chief events in each reign."

Miss Louise, as she was known to the students, was a popular music teacher. She was an exceptional pianist and also taught violin. All the girls in the school participated in a yearly operetta or cantata. Louise taught mathematics as well. Ada and Amy (and perhaps Mrs Maudsay?) carried the remainder of the classes. By all accounts they made learning enjoyable. According to Ramsdale:

> The Maudsleys were all of a genial and tolerant disposition. One delightful way they had of teaching history was by charades. They had brought with them from England great chests full of costumes. The girls dressed themselves up and acted out characters in history.

The class size grew from the first few students to all the students the Maudslay women could handle. Between 1882 and 1890 the Academy's reputation grew until people all over the region considered it the finest place to send their young women for education.

Robert and Harry Maudslay moved west to begin a sheep raising business. Eventually Amy married Doctor George Rice, but died a few years afterwards. Doctor Rice then married Ada and they moved to St. Louis, Missouri. Louise married Herman Thalman whose first wife, Viola, had died in 1881. Louise was still considered a fine pianist when she died in 1950 at the age of 94.

Sources

Dumaresq de Carteret-Bisson, F.S., Captain. <u>Our Schools and Colleges</u>. Simpkin, Marshall, and Company. London. 1884.

> Google search: This entire book is scanned. The entry for Cheetham Collegiate School gives the number of "day pupils" as 300 with 21 boarders, apparently all male students. 150 students

attended "young lady day classes." There was a head master with 25 assistant masters and governesses. This college prep school was located in Manchester, England. Harry and Robert Maudslay attended this school sometime before their sisters taught there.

Guthrie, John. <u>Descriptive Account of Bandera City and Bandera County</u>. Bugle Office. Bandera. 1888.

Hudspeth, William, ed. "Saturday Races." <u>The Bandera Enterprise</u>. January 21, 1886. Bandera. (article transcribed in <u>100 Years In Bandera County</u>)

Hunter, J. Marvin. <u>100 Years In Bandera County: 1853-1953</u>. The Bandera Bulletin. Bandera. 1953.

Kupper, Winifred, ed. <u>Texas Sheepman: The Reminiscences of Robert Maudslay</u>. University of Texas Press. Austin. 1951.

This book spells the family name with an "lay." Other sources spell the name with an "ley."

Ramsdell, Charles. "Bandera—Athens In The Hills." <u>The San Antonio Express</u>. (Circa 1946. The exact date is missing.) Bandera Clipping File. DRT Library. San Antonio.

35

Jailbreak

Anyone picking up the <u>Bandera Bugle</u> in the summer of 1889 would have noticed the prominent front page ad for H.H. Carmichael & Company announcing that the wholesale and retail dealers carried dry goods, groceries, clothing, lumber, shingles, sash doors and blinds. Furthermore, the company was the agent for Weber Wagons. Less noticeably Huffmeyer Brothers' ad stated the availability of Studebaker Wagons at their store. Some sports fans had been following the hype surrounding the heavyweight boxing match between Sullivan and Killrain. In July they learned that Sullivan was victorious in the 72nd round after two hours and 18 minutes. Other readers had been following the continuing story of "Elsa, the Face at the Window." Some may have appreciated that world and national news came through a telegraph service. Local news usually reported that somebody had grown however many bushels of corn and someone else had just shipped some cattle. The local news suddenly became less mundane:

Thursday August 1, 1889

Jailbreak

>Between the hours of eight and nine o'clock on Wednesday evening—supper time—two of the three prisoners confined in our jail succeeded in making good their escape from it. They were not confined to the cages but were at liberty in the corridor, and from this by making a hole through the stone wall they got into the hallway, drew the

latches of the front door burst it open and got off. Graves, one of the prisoners, remained, but Ed. Bonnard (colored) and Kidd, who was only put in on Sunday, and is wanted in Milam County as a horse thief, made good their escape. This is the third similar attempt to break out in this way but the two former attempts were unsuccessful.

The prisoners were in possession of a crowbar which must have been handed in to them through the window.

Sheriff Sanders and constable Parish immediately started in pursuit and it is to be hoped they will be successful in recapturing the fugitives.

Latest.—Before dinner today Jeff Cooksey (colored) was arrested on a charge of complicity with the escaped prisoners.

Constable Parish

R.A. Parish was appointed Bandera County Constable, Precinct One, December 31, 1888.

Sheriff V.P. Sanders

Valerius P. Sanders served as Bandera County Sheriff from 1888-1892.

Schmidtke & Hay/H.H. Carmichael & Company

George Hay was a storekeeper in Bandera City during the Civil War. Uncertain whether he owned his own store at that time, but after the war he partnered with Charles Schmidtke to form Schmidtke & Hay, a general merchandise store. Schmidtke had bought the water-powered saw and grist mill that James, Montel & Company had built before the war. A two-story stone building went up to house the store and saloon.

H.H. Carmichael came to Bandera City as a successful cattleman and bought Charles Schmidtke's interest in the store and mill. New side by side buildings housed the store and saloon. The two-story Schmidtke & Hay building became the county courthouse.

H.H. Carmichael & Company became overextended in the 1890's when they tried to expand into other towns. The company was among several of the early Bandera merchants that were knocked out of business by the Panic of 1893. James B. Hart, Carmichael's book keeper, and George T. Lincoln, a druggist, bought the H.H. Carmichael inventory and opened their own store.

The Jail

Early Bandera County law offenders were held on the honor system or chained to a tree. In the rough post-war times a square cypress structure provided more secure holdings. By the 1880s the court house (the old Schmidtke & Hay building) was barely adequate for county business and a new jail was needed. Well known for his courthouse designs, Alfred Giles worked out the plans for the jail with offices for county officials.

Jeff Cooksey

Six slaves worked the cotton field on the Jack Ranch in the 1850s. Six others were owned in ones or twos by various people around the county. The dozen slaves living in Antebellum Bandera County left the region after the Civil War.

Only gradually in the post war years did cotton become a cash crop for many in the county, whether on a large or small scale. During the 1880s black families settled in the county, finding work in the cotton fields. They formed a community called Newtonville. Readers of the Bugle might have seen the notice that the church there was having an extended meeting and that all were invited. The Cooksey farm was close by, near Tarpley

Pass. Jeff Cooksey, born between 1860 and 1863, was living in Karnes, Texas, for the 1870 census. He served on the Board of Trustees for the Newtonville school 1882 to 1889 and again later in 1899. He had married Gracie Fisher and they called one of their children Jeff Cooksey, Jr.

Also known as Little Jeff Cooksey, he was a muscular and over six feet tall (the appellation distinguished him from his father and did not really relate to his size). Born September 20, 1879, he married Mahalia (Mahala, Mahaley) Thornton and they had five children together. For some time, he worked at the new two-story Lincoln and Hart mercantile store on the corner of Eleventh and Cedar streets.

George Lincoln developed a livestock medicine. Little Jeff made the concoction which they merchandised as Hell For Screw Worms. Hart died in 1914 and Lincoln died in 1917. When Lincoln & Hart closed its doors, Jeff Cooksey, Jr. continued to make and sell the remedy. He died after a farming accident at the age of 45, August 8, 1924. Jeff Cooksey's name continued to be passed down through succeeding generations.

Unknown if the alleged horse thief and his pal were ever apprehended or who actually accused Jeff Cooksey of aiding their escape. The crowbar also remains a mystery, but the following week after the jailbreak, the <u>Bugle</u> reported in Local News:

Thursday August 8, 1889

> Jeff Cooksey, who was arrested on a charge of complicity with the escaped prisoners from jail, after a very short examining trial on Thursday afternoon, was released, it being evident that the charge was "trumped up."

Sources

Edwards, Carolyn. "Early Blacks' 'Footprints' Still Evident." The Bandera Bulletin. February 27, 1991.

Edwards, Carolyn. "Black Students Attended Two Schools." The Bandera Bulletin. March 1, 1991.

Edwards, Carolyn. "Few Markers Remain In Cemetery." The Bandera Bulletin. March 6, 1991.

Election Return. Bandera County. 1888. Archives Division. Texas State Library. Austin.

Guthrie, John, ed. "Jailbreak." The Bandera Bugle. August 1, 1889. Microfilm. Center For American Studies. UT Austin.

Guthrie, John, ed. "Local News." The Bandera Bugle. August 8, 1889. Microfilm. Center For American Studies. UT Austin.

Huffmeyer, Adolf. "Pioneer Merchants of Bandera." Frontier Times. (December 1934) Volume 12, Number 3. Pages 128-135.

Hunter, J. Marvin. 100 Years In Bandera. The Bandera Bulletin. 1953.

Loth, Donna Schultke. Geneological Research on Cooksey Family. Bandera County Genweb Site.

Tobin, Peggy. "Recorded Deaths of Black Persons." The Bandera County Historian. (Summer 1999) Volume 21. Number 2. Page 4.

36

Bulah, the "Lost" County and the Panic of 1893

Bulah County is not on the maps today, but it was once imagined as most of the region that became Real County. During the session of the 24th Legislature of the State of Texas the citizens of Frio Canyon proposed to create a new county from parts of Uvalde, Edwards, and Bandera counties, including the Sabinal Canyon area. Frio Canyon at that time was the western edge of Bandera County across the divide from Sabinal Canyon.

In the mid1850s John Leakey, N.M.C. Patterson and their families were the first to settle in Frio Canyon. In 1868 the Lombardy Irrigation Company was formed by N.M.C. Patterson, W.F. Smith and Theophilus Watkins. The farming community that grew up around the project was known for many years as "The Ditch." In 1875 it became known as Rio Frio.

Settlers from Waresville and Kerrville began moving into Frio Canyon during the late 1870s. They were mostly of Scottish and English extraction. A community formed about ten miles above Rio Frio and became known as Leakey in 1880.

Although in part of Bandera County, the Frio Canyon settlers were somewhat separated from the rest of the county, physically by the rough divide of hills and emotionally and economically by ties to Kerrville. By the mid1890s these people began to think they should form their own county. Unfortunately for their plans, the 1890s were times of great economic uncertainty. The Panic of 1893 devastated businesses all across the

United States, including several in the county seat of Bandera.

The citizens in Sabinal Canyon were not in the mood to be included in the proposed new county. They were familiar with the myriad problems that had beset the construction of the recently finished Bandera County courthouse. They could visualize all sorts of new taxes and bond programs that would be necessary to set up a new county. A protest petition was drawn up in two copies and signed by 64 Sabinal Canyon men.

Eighteen years later the time was right for the formation of the new county, but the name would not be Bulah. The name first proposed was Murphy, but was soon replaced with the name of the popular state senator, Julius Real. The county that finally formed around Frio Canyon included parts of Bandera, Kerr, and Edwards counties. It was organized in 1913 and called Real County after the prominent Hill Country figure. Sabinal Canyon remained as part of the 822 square miles of Bandera County.

37

Julius Real:
A Son of The Hill Country:
1860-1944

German immigrants Caspar and Emilie Real (sister of Charles Schreiner) settled in the Comfort area. Julius Real was born May 7, 1860, on the family ranch on Turtle Creek seven miles south of Kerrville. His education was sporadic through the days of Indian raids. For a short while he attended school in Comfort, at another time the family had a private tutor on the ranch. Later there was a country school a few miles from the ranch. He attended Southwestern University at Georgetown for a couple of years in the early 1880s.

His father's ranch was one of the largest sheep ranches in the region and Julius was kept busy there during his early manhood years. February 23, 1886, he married Marguerethe Koch Schmidt and together they had one child.

Among the elected officials of his time Julius Real was the lone Republican in a Democratic state. He was chairman of the Kerr County Republican Committee for 30 years. In 1894, the year after his father died, he was elected Kerr county commissioner and held that office for eight years. In 1902 he was elected Kerr county judge and county superintendent of schools, holding both positions for the next six years.

In 1908 he defeated John F. Onion of San Antonio in a hotly contested election for the state Senate. He served six years as senator from the 26th Senatorial district: Kerr, Kendall, Bandera and Bexar counties. His district included San Antonio, "the largest and wettest city in the state," at a time when the notion of prohibition of alcohol was in its ascendancy throughout the state and the country. As Chairman of the Finance Committee and of the Land Office Committee and as a member of 11 other committees, he worked hard to represent the interests of his constituents. When interviewed at the Gunther Hotel in San Antonio in 1911, he was ebullient about the prospects of the new railroad being built from there to Fredericksburg and the benefits that would bring to the region. However, the reporter found, "Senator Real did not care to discuss politics, either Republican or Democratic." (The San Antonio, Fredericksburg, and Northern Railway was completed in 1913.)

January 1911, the 32nd Texas Legislature was sharply divided between Pro-state-wide prohibitionists (Drys) and Anti-prohibitionists (Anti's). The Drys hoped to push through their legislative agenda while out-going Dry Governor Thomas M. Campbell was still in office and before the inauguration of the Anti governor-elect Oscar B. Colquitt. The Drys actually had a majority in both houses, but the Anti's outmaneuvered them at every turn. Finally, forestalling a vote just before the inauguration, Julius Real and ten other Anti state senators disappeared from Austin. The newspapers could not report their location and the state senate could not gather a quorum. The missing senators were hiding out in Bandera County. The incident became known as the Whiskey Rebellion and the tactic has been repeated by later generations of Texas legislators.

Successful Texas Republican politicians were rare in those days. While Real was still serving as a State Senator, the Bexar County Republican congressional convention of 1912 nominated him for the 14th Congressional District. The San Antonio Express reported, "It is true that Senator Real has sought to prevent his nomination and declared he would not accept it, but it is pointed out that when first nominated for the State Senate he assumed the same attitude and it was some time before he could be prevailed upon to make the race." Nevertheless, he could not be moved to run for the National Congress.

In 1913 A.M. Kennedy introduced House Bill 706 to form a new county from parts of Edwards, Bandera, and Kerr counties. State Representative Kennedy lobbied for the county to be named after his father-in-law, George W. Murphy of Arkansas. A senate committee chaired by Julius Real was formed to consider the matter. When it was proposed that the new county be named Real, Senator Real resigned from the committee. As the San Antonio Express reported April 1, 1913, the "German vote" prevailed and the county was named after Julius Real.

After his second term as a state senator, Real went back to sheep ranching in Kerr County where he continued to promote the interests of the Hill Country. He was vice president of the Texas Sheep and Goat Raisers Association. (In his later years that association made him honorary vice president.) He was on the board of trustees of the Schreiner Institute and on the board of directors of the Kerrville Chamber of Commerce. He belonged to the Masons, the Rotary Club, and the Order of the Sons of Hermann.

The whole Real family enjoyed music. The Texas Gebrigs Saengerbund Verein, a German singing society, was organized in 1870. Caspar Real was the first president of the society and served 15 years. Julius followed his father as president of the society and served 50 years. Society members came from 10 counties to the annual two-day "Sing Fest" for the program of German and old American songs.

Julius Real: A Son of The Hill Country: 1860 - 1944

Julius Real's interest in nature conservation was reflected in his senate record and in his membership in the Woodmen of the World. Deer hams and hides had been commodities in the region since frontier times and many people supplemented their incomes through deer hunting. A deer could be sold for three dollars, 2 deer hams sold for two dollars and a deer hide would bring one dollar. The scarcity of deer in parts of the Hill Country was becoming noticeable. Between 1913 and 1919 Charles Schreiner provided the financing for Fred Large and Julius Real to go to Austin. The men successfully lobbied for a game law, which required a hunting license and limited the number of deer that could be killed.

During World War I Julius Real served on the Council of Defense. This organization was formed in 1917 at the national, state, and county levels to support the war effort in general and helped with public morale, troop recruitment, and war loan and Red Cross drives. The councils were active until 1919 providing aid to returning soldiers.

In 1924 Real returned to the Texas Senate, serving two more terms. He was known among his senate colleagues as the "Grand Old Man of the Hill Country." He retired from politics in 1929. He was 84 when he died May 29, 1944.

Sources

"All, All, Is Chaos and Confusion." January 14, 1911. The Texas Republic. San Antonio.

Bennett, Bob. Kerr County, Texas: 1856-1956. Naylor. San Antonio. 1956.

"Bitter Fight In Prospect." January 21, 1911. The Texas Republic. San Antonio.

"Drys Again Lose By Anti Senators Breaking Quorum." January 16, 1911. The San Antonio Express. San Antonio.

Garrison, Lora B. Davis. Pioneers In The Frio Canyon Hill Country: An Oral History Study. Copy in DRT Library. San Antonio. 1980?

"It Will Be Real County." April 1, 1913. The San Antonio Express. San Antonio.

Lewis, Grace L. "Creation and Organization [of Real County]." The Bandera County Historian. (Spring 1992) Volume 14. Number 1. Pages 6-7.

Murray, Myrtle. "Casper Real." The Cattleman. (1938) Volume. Number. Pages 51-54.

Obituary. The Cattleman. (July 1944) Volume 31. Number 2. Page 42.

"Railroad Is Certainty." October 2, 1911. The San Antonio Express. San Antonio.

"Real Defeats Onion." November 4, 1908. The San Antonio Express. San Antonio.

"Real Is Chosen Opponent For Jas. L. Sladen." August 25, 1912. The San Antonio Express. San Antonio.

"Real Nominated For State Senate." The Pioneer. (November 1924) Volume 5. Number 6. Page 25.

"Turmoil of Last Session Missing Now." January 20, 1913. The Austin Statesman. Austin.

Tylor, Ron, et al, eds. The New Handbook of Texas.

38

The Woman of the Western Star
Adapted by Earl Hardin Jr.

In the summer of 1844 a ranger company had fought Indians near Bandera Pass. The Indians were defeated and retreated to the north. The rangers were too exhausted to follow and rode southeast to put what they felt was a safe distance between themselves and the Indians. As they made camp near Polly's Peak, darkness was approaching, a full moon was rising, and a mockingbird was singing its last notes of the day. The rangers had gathered around their campfire about to begin their traditional story-telling hour, when suddenly the mockingbird became silent and the air seemed eerily still. The alert rangers were all eyes and ears as they sensed something unusual and suspected Indians lurking about. The breeze came up again and a cloud momentarily passed across the moon. The sun was well below the horizon now and as the cloud passed, the rising moon shown brightly on a beautiful apparition in the rangers' midst. She was a tall Indian woman with long braided hair. A leather band around her forehead glistened with sparkling crystal beads. Her neck was adorned with strings of colored beads and a shell necklace. The fringes of a shimmering blue skirt reached nearly to her ankles. A bead-embroidered quiver hung at her side. Across her back was a bow of bois d'arc. She stood there with her arms folded in calm, but defiant majesty. The rangers were awed and it was some time before their captain could stammer, "Where do you come from and why are you here alone?"

In a confident and commanding tone she replied, "I come alone because I know not fear: The Great Spirit is my father. I have come to ask that there be peace between your people and mine, for it should be so among all peoples." She then set three ornately carved and painted arrows at her feet. The arrowheads were of polished obsidian and gleamed in the moonlight. The white blooms of yucca plants on either side of her seemed to glow as the woman turned her head to the night sky. She pointed to a brilliant star in the west and said, "That star is my home. I go there now." Unnoticed by the mystified rangers, a dark cloud had gathered above Polly's Peak. Suddenly, there was a blinding flash of lightning with nerve-shattering thunder and the woman was gone. The men stood in shocked paralysis. All was still and quiet. Finally the plaintive notes of a whippoorwill broke the silence. The men roused themselves and grabbed their weapons. Some prepared for defense, while the captain sent others in pairs to scout about the vicinity. When they were certain there were no Indians or anyone else for miles about, they gathered around the fire again and tried to make some sense of what they had just experienced. Some kept looking for the three arrows, but they were not to be found.

> *This story dates at least to the 1880s and has been attributed to Hugh Duffy who settled in Bandera County in the 1860s. He said he heard the story from an old ranger, but perhaps Duffy, well-known in his time as a storyteller, is the originator. The Texas Folk-Lore Society has published a version of the story as written by Adele B. Looscan.*

www.ingramcontent.com/pod-product-compliance
Lightning Source LLC
Chambersburg PA
CBHW071309110526
44591CB00010B/843